THE TRUTH ABOUT
SUCCESS AND MOTIVATION

THE TRUTH ABOUT SUCCESS AND MOTIVATION

ADVICE ON HOW TO BE ONE OF LIFE'S WINNERS

Bob Montgomery

THORSONS PUBLISHING GROUP

The author and publisher thank Professor R. W. Novaco of the Department of Social Ecology, University of California, for permission to reproduce Novaco's Dimensions of Anger Reactions scale (page 17). The table on pages 36–7 is reproduced by special permission of the Publisher, Consulting Psychologists Press Inc., Palo Alto, CA 94306, from the State Trait Anxiety Inventory, Form Y, by Charles Spielberger and Associates © 1977. Further reproduction is prohibited without the Publisher's consent.

First UK edition published 1988
Originally published by
Lothian Publishing Company Pty Ltd
11 Munro Street Port Melbourne Victoria 3207 in 1987

British Library Cataloguing in Publication Data

Montgomery, Bob
    The truth about success and motivation:
    plain advice on how to be one of life's
    real winners.
    1. Personal success-manuals
    I. Title
    158.'1

    ISBN 0-7225-1637-1

*Published by Thorsons Publishers Limited,
Wellingborough, Northamptonshire, NN8 2RQ, England*

Printed in Great Britain by
Richard Clay Limited, Bungay, Suffolk

    3   5   7   9   10   8   6   4   2

CONTENTS

1 | THE BARNUM-AND-BAILEY, DEATH-OR-GLORY THEORY OF SUCCESS

If I asked you to point out some of the people you see as good examples of success and motivation, the chances are that you would choose prominent people, the ones who turn up in the news and on TV, the wealthy businessperson, the gold medal athlete, the media personality, the quoted politician, the super salesperson. Well, the first piece of truth I can share with you is that I have seen enough prominent people close up to be sure that many of them are unhappy, driven people who often see themselves as failures. If being successful includes being happy — reasonably happy most of the time — and enjoying life — reasonable enjoyment most of the time — then prominence is not a reliable indicator of success.

But prominent people are often described as 'successful' and 'motivated'. Why? Because most of us have been fooled by popular myths, by frauds, and by our human fallibility. If I am going to help you to find true success and motivation, I first need to demonstrate how you, too, have probably been fooled, so that you set out with realistic goals.

There is another reason for disposing of the 'prominence' equals 'success' myth, a reason I see as very important. In my clinical work, I have been struck by how often a lack of self-esteem underlies so many problems. Unconfident people are scared to live successfully; people who don't love themselves cannot successfully love others. So much unhappiness arises from people being taught to see themselves as failing when realistically they did not. The 'prominence' myth is a *mean* view of success. How many prominent people do you know? How many have you even met? If you have to be prominent to be successful, then very few people will be allowed to be successful. A society that equates prominence with success is a *mean* society, miserly with its recognition.

I believe success is for everybody, not just the prominent few. (In fact, many of them could use a dose of real success.) Every one of us can be truly successful. Every one of us can be well motivated. To get to the truth of that, let's get rid of the lies.

The Barnum-and-Bailey approach to success

Here we go again. Here's yet another American getting off the plane and offering (for a mere pittance of one or two hundred dollars) to teach us the secrets of success in a one-day seminar (with lunch in a plush hotel included, of course, and the opportunity to buy the great man's collected wisdom on a glorious colour video-tape at a personal discount). If these Cecil B. de Mille spectaculars are all they are cracked up to be, I can't help wondering why the same participants seem to keep going back for more. If you learned the secrets of success at your first seminar, why would you need a second one?

Now, don't get me wrong. Some of my best friends are Americans. And some of the best psychological research is done by Americans. But P. T. Barnum was also an American, and some of his latter-day countrymen seem to have adopted his well-known adage: 'There's a sucker born every minute'. Yesterday's snake oil salesman has been followed, in many cases, by today's success and motivation seminar speaker. Their material is certainly presented slickly. P. T. Barnum would have been proud of the three ring razzle dazzle. No doubt the high price tag on each seminar cashes in on the bitter medicine myth: 'If it costs this much to hear this guy, he *must* be good.'

I have been dismayed by the willingness of some of the business people I know, each a real success in his field of activity, to accept as gospel the lightweight nonsense peddled by some of the 'experts' who trip around the seminar circuit. In trying to understand why these people who are definitely not fools were being parted from their money so easily, I have realized how easy it is to dazzle people with a good show and a plausible presentation that is outside their own fields of knowledge and expertise.

The trouble is, we don't think logically. No, you don't. I know you have been told to and I am sure you would like to think you do, but the truth is, you don't, at least not much of the time. Human brains are not designed, have not evolved, for logical thinking. Humans can learn logic, as an artificial exercise, much as you can teach a parrot to talk. Step into the nearest jungle and you won't find many parrots talking. Step out into the street and you won't find many people thinking logically.

This is just as well, or we wouldn't be here. Real logic is ponderously slow, partly because it lacks any common sense. If our original ancestor, stepping out of her cave one prehistoric morning and coming face to face with a sabre-toothed tiger, had tried to solve this problem *logically*, she would first have had to list all possible paths of action — including many that common sense would tell you were not worth considering, like 'Wait for the next Ice Age' or 'Hang about until sabre-toothed tigers are extinct' — and then she would have had to weigh up the pros and cons of each possibility, including the obviously silly ones, and somewhere in the middle of this lengthy process she would have been tiger food. That's real logic: great for remorselessly tracking down the right answer, if you have all day.

What our ancestor actually did was to take one look at the tiger and think: 'The last animal I saw like that tried to eat me! Quick, run like hell!' She was thinking plausibly, not logically, and that's why there are still humans around. Plausible thinking has the advantage of being much faster than logic, while still being mostly right. Plausible thinking is what our brains do naturally. Something looks plausible to me, given my present attitudes and past experiences, I accept it. In the process I will sometimes make logical mistakes, because plausible thinking is very influenced by superficial appearances (a fact long since recognized by the advertising industry), but to make those mistakes by thinking plausibly rather than logically is just to be human.

The seminar industry has also recognized the acceptance given to plausible appearances. You will notice that my plausible thinking depends a lot on my past experiences. So present me with something that I have not experienced before, and I am less able to judge it realistically. Present it glossily, plausibly, and I may well accept it. Throw in a few anecdotes that I do recognize and identify with, even if they are not *logically* related to your main proposal, and I am quite likely to accept it. That's the key to pop psychology:

it sounds enough like you at a few points for you to accept all of the other points, especially if they are new to you.

Now, here's a problem. If your thinking is vulnerable to being fooled by plausibly presented gobbledegook in areas you have not much experience in, and you have not had the chance to learn many of the facts about success and motivation, how do you tell when you are looking at gobbledegook and when you are looking at facts? Fortunately, there is a way.

A couple of years ago I was invited to be guest speaker at a conference of an organization exclusively for successful business leaders and I sat through a 90-minute presentation by one of the American seminar stars. By the end of his talk, I figured he had covered five basic psychological facts, and got two of them wrong. The audience thought he was great, and even gave him a standing ovation. I was puzzled: these people were no dummies. To belong to their organization, you had to have really made it in business. Yet here were these smart people bedazzled by plausibly presented gobbledegook. That was when I first realized how much people could be swayed by a slick presentation of ideas outside their own areas of expertise. Only later, while catching up on research in cognitive (or thinking) psychology, did I learn about the human tendency to think plausibly rather than logically.

That evening we all trooped off to a conference dinner. Sitting with members of the organization, I was put on the spot when some of them said they thought this particular talk had been wonderful, and didn't I agree? How was I to say what I honestly thought of the talk, without just sounding like the local boy, envious of the Amercian high flier? Finally I asked them a question: 'Tell me what you will do tomorrow, that you didn't do yesterday, as a result of hearing that talk today?' They looked puzzled, they still insisted it had been a 'wonderful presentation', but none of them could actually indicate a practical outcome of having heard that American.

You can apply this same test to advertising to see whether you have been told the truth about a product or fed some glossy, plausible bunk. Does it work? After your next success and motivation seminar (or tape, or book, including this one), ask yourself the following. Did I actually receive any *practical* advice? Do I now have a clear idea of what I should *do*, or do *differently*? If it sounded great, but leaves you with nothing new to try, then it was pop psychology. If you did get some new ideas to try, when you do, *do they work*? If they do, are the resulting gains *worth the price* of the seminar? If the new ideas didn't work, or weren't really worth the price, then P. T. Barnum just got you.

The death-or-glory theory of success

Most of us were first introduced to the concept of winning through playing games, including competitive sports. Coaches and sports teachers are fond of telling you youngsters how these games are meant to prepare us 'for the great game of life'. It's a notion I saw expressed again in a recent issue of an airline in-flight magazine, in an article in which the old tennis/football/cricket star claimed that being successful in sport had prepared them for success in life. Shades of Rudyard Kipling, and the playing fields of England preparing you to save the Empire!

The analogy between sport and the rest of life breaks down on a crucial point and, as a result, the attitudes we learn through sport will be inappropriate for almost all of the rest of our lives (except for more sport). The point is that competitive sports are zero-sum games, while most of life is not. A zero-sum game is one where you can only win if someone else loses: I win one, you lose one, so together our outcomes add up to zero. This includes most parlour games, like cards or board games, and all competitive sports. To have a winner, you must have losers; to be a winner, you must beat others. Apart from the occasional draw, this is all perfectly true for zero-sum games and, if you want to be successful in that sort of activity, you should be trying to win. To be successful in zero-sum games, a competitive approach is best.

The trouble is that most human dealings and relationships are not zero-sum games. In most of the situations you will work, play and live in, it is not necessary for someone else to lose in order for you to win. To be successful, you don't have to beat anybody. In most human situations, it is possible for everybody involved to win, for all to be successful. 'But,' you may be thinking, 'I'm not reading this book to help everybody else to be successful. I want *me* to be successful.'

Good, then pay attention. I think that's a perfectly reasonable goal. I am all in favour of being healthily self-centred, while avoiding the risk of being meanly selfish. I definitely believe your first obligation is to run your life successfully for yourself, because then you will be better able to offer others an honest square deal. Turn yourself inside out, accept things in your life that are plainly wrong for you, for the most noble reasons of self-sacrifice, and eventually you will fall apart and not be able to keep up the act. Then every-body else has the right to ask, 'If that wasn't what you wanted, why didn't you say so?' Say so. Right from the start. Do what is basically right for you, without being unreasonably unfair to others, and then what you offer others is really you. It's what you can expect to be able to deliver consistently, not a phony act. So I am all in favour of you having your personal success high on your agenda, coupled with reasonable respect for the rights and feelings of others. The fact that by being realistically successful as an individual means you will also help others to be successful is a pleasant bonus, a cherry on the ice-cream of your personal success. The aim of this book is to help you to be a real winner in life, not everybody's fairy godmother.

The death-or-glory theory of success, that success equals winning equals beating others, is very pervasive in our culture. Certainly it is pushed hard by the seminar showpeople, who trumpet on about 'being a winner' and 'looking after No.1' (by putting everybody else last). But it has wider popularity than just amongst seminar-goers. I have been surprised how readily some people want to make any activity into a competition. 'Hey, you can put planks under your feet and slide down on snow and it's fun!' 'Sounds great. Let's see who can do it fastest!'

Perhaps it's because we are such a nation of sports-watchers (unfortunately few of us are sports-players) that we so readily accept the extension of zero-sum game principles to the rest of life. Maybe because we believe it is important for our local football team to be successful by beating others, we also believe *we* have to be successful in the same way. At this point in the discussion, some-one usually wants to argue that humans are 'naturally' competitive, that it's the inevitable consequence of our evolution and the applica-tion of the law of survival of the fittest. They will usually cite two stags clashing head on, to win the right to mate with the females. 'See,' the argument goes, 'competition means the best, the tough-est genes are passed on, thus ensuring the survival of the species.'

Once again, it's a poor analogy, because it ignores the major-ity of deer behaviour, which is not competitive, but which also serves the survival of the species. It also ignores the fact that such competitions for mates are usually very ritualized, with a mutually acceptable surrender signal, so that little real harm is done, despite all the huffing and puffing. It's a pity we can't say the same about a lot of human fighting. And most importantly, it ignores the fact that much of human competitiveness is learned, not inherited.

How many times did you witness a classroom scene like this? Teacher looks around the room and fixes his gaze on Charlie: 'Charlie, I want you to tell us all what the square root of 121 is.' Charlie goes pale, then red with embarrassment, struggles in his head, but says nothing. Over the other side of the room, Edwina is nearly climbing out of her seat with eagerness, waving her arm in the air, and saying, 'Sir, sir!' Eventually teacher, with a look of impatience at Charlie, turns to Edwina and says, 'OK, Edwina, what is it?' 'Eleven,' she bursts. 'Right,' says teacher, 'I hope you will do better next time, Charlie.'

To many people Edwina was successful — a winner. She got it right, she was rewarded with the teacher's approval, and she beat the competition, her classmates. But anthropologists would tell you that, to a Hopi Indian, Edwina's behaviour was shameful. To a Hopi, to win like that, at someone else's obvious expense, would be grossly unacceptable behaviour. The point I am making is not that we should necessarily think like Hopi Indians, although in Chapter 9 I will explain why I am glad that teachers nowadays are less likely to act like the one above. The point is that the Hopi definition of success is not a competitive one, yet the Hopi are humans like the rest of us. If competition was 'natural' in some biologically inherited way, then it would turn up in all cultures, and it doesn't. Indeed, cross-cultural research comes up with a bewildering variety of definitions of personal success. The meaning of success is something you learn from your culture, and I believe our culture has taught us badly.

Again, don't get me wrong. I am not objecting to competitive sports or other zero-sum games. They can be pleasant idle amusements or even healthy recreation. I have quite enjoyed the competitive sports and games I have occasionally dabbled in, and I doubt that I was significantly harmed by the experience. What I do object to is the over-simple application of zero-sum attitudes to the non-zero-sum majority of life. The myth that success equals winning equals beating others is dangerous, not only to your health (which would be bad enough) but also to your real success rate. If you swallow that myth, then you will live with a competitive interpersonal style and that means, as I will explain in the next chapter, you will not be nearly as successful as you could have been.

2 | CUT-THROAT COMPETITION: WHOSE THROAT?

Would you describe yourself, or would you like to be able to describe yourself, as:

- ambitious and on the move
- hard-working
- not inclined to sit or lie around and just loaf
- willing to work evenings or weekends to keep ahead
- able to present your point of view clearly and forcefully
- always looking for new challenges to tackle
- unwilling to tolerate inefficiency or incompetence in others?

Yes, indeed, you could be the model of the rising executive, the worker destined for success, praised by the boss, selected for promotion, and nearly ready for your first heart attack. Whoops, what was that last bit? What's so successful about being the first person on your block to have a heart attack? What indeed?

The Type A behaviour pattern

The profile listed above, with which I hope you do not identify, is known as the Type A Behaviour Pattern, sometimes mistakenly called the 'Type A Personality'. These are the people often called 'workaholics' because of their apparent addiction to work, to the neglect and detriment of everything else in their lives. In the original research by two American heart specialists, Dr Meyer Friedman and Dr Ray Rosenman, they concluded that having the Type A Behaviour Pattern doubled your risk of a heart attack. Further they found that it doubled the risk to your heart from other risk factors, like smoking, obesity or excessive drinking.

The research that led to the discovery of the Type A Behaviour Pattern is interesting. Most people are at least vaguely aware of the classic heart risk factors: smoking habits, eating habits, drinking habits, exercise habits, and have heard of some of the consequences of these, such as blood cholesterol and triglyceride levels. You may even have had the latter checked by your doctor and, as a result, been told to change some of the former. (By the way, how did you go? Being told to change your smoking, eating, drinking or exercise is a long way from effectively doing so.

But you have probably heard of someone's Uncle Fred who smoked like a chimney, ate like a pig, drank like a fish, never exercised and lived to be 105. To add to the confusion, you may also have heard of someone's neighbour, who never smoked or drank, ate only vegetables, was thin as a rake, and ran ten kilometres every morning, but had a heart attack at 35! These are the sort of anecdotes usually trotted out by people to justify not trying to lead a healthier lifestyle, an excuse which breaks down on two major points. First, it assumes you have the same degree of genetic risk as Uncle Fred had, and that's rather like playing Russian roulette with your health. Second, it ignores the Type A Behaviour Pattern.

Some individuals, and even some national groups, are high on the classic heart risk factors and yet low on heart disease. Apart from a possible genetic contribution, the major explanation for this seems to be that they are also low on the Type A Behaviour Pattern. The converse of the Type A is the Type B Behaviour Pattern, which is a more relaxed, less competitive or hostile approach to life, like Uncle Fred's (especially after his bottle of rum each night). It is the Western, industrialized countries that have a rising rate of heart disease, despite growing interest in health issues, because it is our cultures, with their strong emphasis on individual competition, that encourage the Type A Behaviour Pattern. I have heard of people boasting that they have the 'Type A Personality' (their use of this incorrect term shows how little they actually know about it) and some of our business leaders are on public record as expecting their employees, especially their executives, to behave like this.

What problem?

People with the Type A Behaviour Pattern usually reject the suggestion that acting like that is a problem, at least until they have their first heart attack. Since 30 per cent of them won't survive that event, it's neither a cost-effective way of doing health education (you have to pay their insurance, support their widows, and train their replacements), nor a hallmark of successful living. The problem is exacerbated by the encouragement of their employers to keep up the Type A Behaviour Pattern. They both share the delusion that being like that is productive. Jumping around like a grasshopper on a hotplate, people with the Type A Behaviour Pattern may *look* productive but, in my experience, that is not as true as they would hope. The thumbnail sketch of the Type A Behaviour Pattern is of someone who is trying to do an increasing number of things in a diminishing amount of time, and it shows. Typically they are over-committed and over-stretched and in fact less truly productive than they could be if they were to approach their work more realistically. Even the ones who are held up as examples of success will usually be successful only in their work — and later I will point out how narrow that criterion is — and even then they are seen as successful because they work better than others, and we are back to competition as the means of being successful. So, what's wrong with that?

Despite their usual reluctance, I do see in therapy some people with the Type A Behaviour Pattern. Sometimes they turn up after surviving their first heart attack; sometimes someone has bullied them into coming before their first heart attack; sometimes their aggressiveness is driving everybody else up the wall. Often they have been dragged in by their spouses, who are desperately trying to save the marriage. They are awful to be married to, a fact that has been confirmed for women at least, in research by psychologists Debra Weaver and Darlene Shaw at the Medical University of South Carolina. They found that in general Type A women have less successful marriages than do Type B women, especially if they are married to a Type A man rather than a Type B. Unfortunately, the incidence of the Type A Behaviour Pattern amongst women seems to be increasing, as more women choose jobs before marriage, and some of them confuse behaving in stereotypically masculine ways with being liberated and successful. Whether it's she or he or both with the Type A Pattern, it's all too often the case of the absent spouse. He (or increasingly often she) is either physically absent because he's still at work, or even when he is at home he's emotionally absent, because his mind is still at work. If you do manage to make contact, he is likely to be worn out or angry because, 'You don't appreciate that he only does it all for you and the kids,' or she objects that, 'You are stifling her personal growth and you are threatened by her success.'

However reluctantly they come, some of these people do eventually realize that what I am saying about the dangers of the Type A Behaviour Pattern, to health, relationships and productivity, does apply to them and my suggestions are in their own best interests. I have been emphasizing that the problem is not a 'personality type' that you might believe you are stuck with, but a behaviour pattern that you can change, providing you want to and someone shows you how to. You provide the first factor, the wish to change, and we provide the second factor, concrete suggestions on how to do so successfully. This has been our stress-management programme, as set out in *You & Stress* (by me and Lynette Evans, published by Nelson), with an emphasis on realistic goals, performance standards, and expectations of others' reactions to you. The need to emphasize realistic thinking in these areas came from my observation that underlying every Type A Behaviour Pattern I have ever seen was a lack of self-esteem. People with Type A Behaviour Pattern feel in perpetual competition and therefore conflict with the rest of the world, frantically trying to prove their personal worth by doing better than others. Since they themselves do not believe in their personal worth, no matter how well they do, it won't be good enough. So they push themselves ever harder, because of their unrealistically impossible definition of success. Success to the Type A is the carrot on a stick that the donkey can never reach.

'Get out of the way, fool!'

Proper diagnosis of the Type A Behaviour Pattern does require a special interview, although you can get an idea of whether or not you are tending that way by completing the test on page 13. Have a try at it now.

How did you go? Time to start some rethinking? Actually, I have found a very simple test that spots the Type A Pattern quite well: when you are driving in traffic, how often do you get angry or impatient with other drivers? Driving really seems to bring out the core flavour of the Type A Pattern, both its competitiveness — 'I must get there faster' — and its hostility — everyone else is a fool who means to block or frustrate your rapid progress. The driver who rushes away at the green light, who weaves in and out of the traffic to try to make up a few seconds, who reacts aggressively to

BEHAVIOURAL
SELF-DESCRIPTIONS

*Below are nineteen scales, each with two possible self-descriptions,
one at each end. Describe how you usually behave by putting a
cross on one of the spaces in each scale, to indicate where your
behaviour would usually be on that scale.*

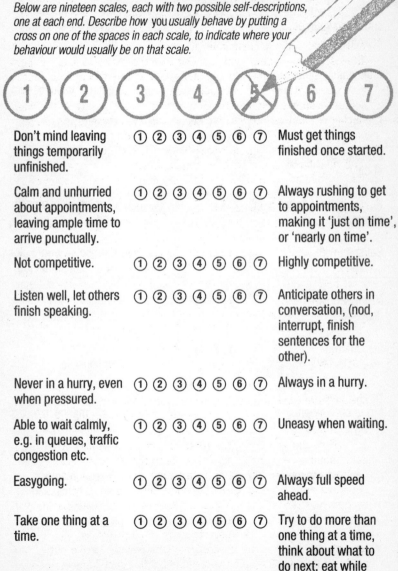

Don't mind leaving things temporarily unfinished.	① ② ③ ④ ⑤ ⑥ ⑦	Must get things finished once started.
Calm and unhurried about appointments, leaving ample time to arrive punctually.	① ② ③ ④ ⑤ ⑥ ⑦	Always rushing to get to appointments, making it 'just on time', or 'nearly on time'.
Not competitive.	① ② ③ ④ ⑤ ⑥ ⑦	Highly competitive.
Listen well, let others finish speaking.	① ② ③ ④ ⑤ ⑥ ⑦	Anticipate others in conversation, (nod, interrupt, finish sentences for the other).
Never in a hurry, even when pressured.	① ② ③ ④ ⑤ ⑥ ⑦	Always in a hurry.
Able to wait calmly, e.g. in queues, traffic congestion etc.	① ② ③ ④ ⑤ ⑥ ⑦	Uneasy when waiting.
Easygoing.	① ② ③ ④ ⑤ ⑥ ⑦	Always full speed ahead.
Take one thing at a time.	① ② ③ ④ ⑤ ⑥ ⑦	Try to do more than one thing at a time, think about what to do next; eat while working.

Slow and deliberate in speech.	① ② ③ ④ ⑤ ⑥ ⑦	Vigorous and forceful in speech (use a lot of gestures).
Concerned with satisfying yourself, not others.	① ② ③ ④ ⑤ ⑥ ⑦	Want recognition by others for a job well done.
Slow doing things.	① ② ③ ④ ⑤ ⑥ ⑦	Fast doing things (eating, walking, etc.).
Easygoing.	① ② ③ ④ ⑤ ⑥ ⑦	Hard driving.
Express feelings openly.	① ② ③ ④ ⑤ ⑥ ⑦	Hold feelings in.
Have a large number of interests.	① ② ③ ④ ⑤ ⑥ ⑦	Few interests outside work.
Satisfied with job.	① ② ③ ④ ⑤ ⑥ ⑦	Ambitious, want quick advancement on job.
Never set own deadlines.	① ② ③ ④ ⑤ ⑥ ⑦	Often set own deadlines.
Feel limited responsibility.	① ② ③ ④ ⑤ ⑥ ⑦	Always feel responsible.
Never judge things in terms of numbers.	① ② ③ ④ ⑤ ⑥ ⑦	Often judge performance in terms of numbers, (how many; how much).
Casual about work.	① ② ③ ④ ⑤ ⑥ ⑦	Take work very seriously (work weekends, bring work home).

T O T A L :

INTERPRETING BEHAVIOURAL
SELF-DESCRIPTIONS SCORES

Add up the nineteen numbers you have put crosses on to get your total score.

TOTAL	INDICATIONS
110-140	Marked Type A Behaviour Pattern; possibly high coronary heart disease risk, especially if over 40 or smoking
80-109	Moderate Type A Behaviour Pattern; possibly coronary heart disease prone
60-79	Mixture of Type A Behaviour Pattern and Type B Behaviour Pattern; recognize risk of increasing A
30-59	Moderate Type B Behaviour Pattern; probably relaxed and coping, with less risk of coronary heart disease
19-29	Marked Type B Behaviour Pattern; probably low risk of coronary heart disease

anyone impeding her progress, is very probably suffering from the Type A Behaviour Pattern.

The research identifying the Type A Behaviour Pattern as a major risk to your heart has been around now for some ten years and, like all scientific research, it has been undergoing some critical review and extension. After all, not all busy people have heart attacks. If you look again at the above description of the Pattern you will realize it is something of a hotch-potch of behaviours, some mental, some verbal, some physical. It is something of a blunt instrument. Researchers at the Duke University Medical Centre in North Carolina have been trying to refine the Pattern, to identify the key risk elements and have now pinpointed one, hostility. They found that the Type A Pattern did allow them to predict coronary disease, but so also did measures of hostility. In fact, hostility levels gave a better prediction of coronary artery blockage than did measures of the Type A Pattern.

So, some of us busy people may heave a great sigh of relief. It seems possible to be busy in a Type A style without necessarily risking our hearts. However, before you take that as permission to bury yourself even more deeply in your work, I would point out that the Duke researchers focused on the risk of conorary disease. It is still quite possible that leading an imbalanced, Type A lifestyle could offer other risks to your health and it certainly imposes a severe strain on your marriage and family relationships. Even if you decide your ticker is safe inside your tranquil breast, you may decide to revise some aspects of your lifestyle for other, equally important reasons.

And some of us had better get even more worried, preferably constructively. If you think you tend to feel hostile towards others reasonably often, then your heart may be at risk, whether or not you have developed the Type A Pattern. You can get an indication of how much this may apply to you by completing the test on page 17 designed by Professor Ray Novaco. Have a go at it now.

There are no numerical norms for this test like those for the behavioural self-descriptions. I interpret the results by taking as problematic any score of four or more. The more of the seven items you have rated yourself at four or more, the bigger the problem you are having with anger and so presumably the more risk for your coronary arteries. Psychologists at the Eckerd College in Florida found that hostile people who tended to bottle up their anger were at risk of having blocked coronary arteries. But others at the University of Maryland found that, amongst young patients at least, those who expressed their anger outwards were also at risk. So it seems that it's hostile anger that is the key, especially cynical hostility, according to the Duke researchers. My hunch is that this life-threatening, cynically hostile attitude towards others, marked by general suspicion and mistrust, results from having swallowed the success = winning = beating others myth, as I will explain shortly, so working on the suggestions in this book could be reducing your cardiac risk, too. I repeat, I cannot see anything successful in having a heart attack.

One other important point emerged from the Duke Center research. They found that the degree of narrowing of a hostile person's coronary arteries reflected how little social support he usually had. It would seem that having people who offer you emotional support can reduce the harmful effects of your hostility, while an absence of such support leaves you more vulnerable to those effects. This suggests that having successful relationships with your spouse and others is not only a component of personal suc-

DIMENSIONS OF ANGER REACTIONS

Do your best to judge as accurately as you can the degree to which the following statements describe your feelings and behaviour. That is, rate the degree to which each statement applies to you.

0	1	2	3	4	5	6	7	8
NOT AT ALL	VERY LITTLE	A LITTLE	SOME, NOT MUCH	MODERATE-LY SO	FAIRLY MUCH	MUCH	VERY MUCH	EXACTLY SO

1 I often find myself getting angry at people or situations.
⓪ ① ② ③ ④ ⑤ ⑥ ⑦ ⑧

2 When I do get angry, I get really mad.
⓪ ① ② ③ ④ ⑤ ⑥ ⑦ ⑧

3 When I get angry, I stay angry.
⓪ ① ② ③ ④ ⑤ ⑥ ⑦ ⑧

4 When I get angry at someone, I want to hit or clobber the person.
⓪ ① ② ③ ④ ⑤ ⑥ ⑦ ⑧

5 My anger interferes with my ability to get my work done.
⓪ ① ② ③ ④ ⑤ ⑥ ⑦ ⑧

6 My anger prevents me from getting along with people as well as I'd like to.
⓪ ① ② ③ ④ ⑤ ⑥ ⑦ ⑧

7 My anger has had a bad effect on my health.
⓪ ① ② ③ ④ ⑤ ⑥ ⑦ ⑧

cess, but contributes to other aspects of your success, like staying alive, and that adds importance to the relationship skills in Chapters 4 and 5 and my suggestions in Chapters 8 and 9.

Success = winning = beating others?

The problem with this myth is that, if you adopt it as your criterion for success, you *must* fail, most if not all of the time. You wind up believing you are only successful at something when you do it better than everybody else. Your yardstick for determining success is to compare yourself with others, frantically hoping you have beaten everybody. You can't. Let's say you *are* the world's best piano player (or insurance salesperson, or whatever). I'm not sure how you would ever really determine this, but let's imagine you did, and you were summoned to the United Nations to receive the world's accolade for playing pianos (or selling insurance or whatever). So? I'll bet you are not also the world's best cook, tennis player, metal worker, spouse, parent, etc., etc. What's more, I'll bet that if you ever did get to be world champion at anything, you did it by leading such a lop-sided lifestyle that in fact you did rather badly at most other parts of your life. That's not my definition of success.

In fact, most of us will never be world champions at anything and that's important. If you tell yourself you are successful only when you have beaten everybody else, then you must fail, in your own eyes, because sooner or later you must bump into somebody who does it better than you, regardless of what 'it' is. And that's the trap of adopting external criteria for success: you *must* fail, because sooner or later you will find someone who can beat you, someone who plays the piano better, or sells more insurance, or cooks better, or has a faster car or a bigger house. You may have done very well, by any realistic judgement, but you will be telling yourself you 'failed', because someone else did it better.

Of course, that's what the competitive sports approach to life is all about. It doesn't matter how well *you* think you did, what matters is the evaluation of the judge (or the referee or the audience or who ever else was watching). So get out there into the great game of life and pack death at the possibility that someone may beat you. Run, run, and you will earn your Type A Behaviour Pattern yet! Who would want the *shame* of coming second? Well, that kind of thinking accounts for the driven, competitive nature of the Type A Behaviour Pattern, but why is it also so hostile and aggressive?

Simple, since you are out to prove yourself by beating every-body else, you *know* that they are out to do the same to you. Everybody is a challenger. Anybody who does anything you do, especially anybody who does it at all well, is a potential rival and must be treated as such. The person in the car next to yours may look as if he doesn't care who gets to the next red light first, but *you* know he does and you aren't going to let him beat you. Even those who are not in obvious competition with you can be a threat to your success, by getting in the way. The buffoon in the car in front of you may not actually be competing with you, but she is blocking your lightning take-off and so is equally deserving of your anger. Or all of those incompetents who work with or for you, who won't adopt the perfectionist standards that after all are only what you expect of yourself. Why won't they get a move on or get out of the way?

And there you are, trapped. No, not by them, but by your-self, by your attitudes, by your external criteria for success, trapped into forever comparing yourself, and therefore competing with others. And that means you will miss out on a lot of success.

Co-operation versus competition

Professor Robert Axelrod, a political scientist at the University of Michigan, has led research into the comparison of co-operative and competitive strategies, using a simulated situation called the pris-oner's dilemma. The situation has been varied a bit in different research but basically it goes like this: you and a fellow prisoner have been accused of committing a crime and you are being interro-gated separately. If you both keep silent — if you co-operate with each other — you can both get off scot-free. On the other hand, if you betray your partner, you go free while he gets a prison sen-tence. Likewise, if he betrays you, he goes free while you get the prison sentence. The trap is that, if you both betray each other, you both get a prison sentence. That's your dilemma: do you trust your partner in the hope that you can both get off, or do you not trust your partner and go for what you think is best for just you, regard-less of how that affects your partner? You will realize this is a non-zero-sum game: you could both win, if you co-operate, or one of you could win, at least the first time around, by being selfishly competitive. After that first round, of course, it's doubtful that your partner would trust you again.

The greatest interest has been in studies where the game is played repeatedly, for points rather than prison sentences, and the question has been, what kind of strategy wins the most? The answer has been very clear: co-operation consistently wins more than competition. In one very elaborate study, people were invited to write computer programmes to play the game, to see if there was some clever way of beating the competition. All sorts of elaborate programmes were submitted, employing a wide range of strategies for beating the competition. Some of these programmes would always betray their opponent, some would betray sometimes, and some used complicated statistics to decide whether or not to betray. One programme consistently won more than all of the others: simple co-operation.

The simple co-operation strategy was called 'Tit for Tat' because it rested on simple reciprocity: it did to its opponent whatever its opponent had just done to it. If the opponent co-operated on the last trial, Tit for Tat co-operated this time. If the opponent betrayed on the last trial, Tit for Tat betrayed this time. When aggressive, competitive programmes were pitted against Tit for Tat, they did not lose but, apart from their first trial at betrayal, they did not win either, because Tit for Tat would match them. When they were pitted against each other, they did very badly, because the mutual aggression just escalated. When a more flexible programme was pitted against Tit for Tat, it could quickly learn the benefits of co-operation, because Tit for Tat is such a transparently obvious strategy. In a sense it says, very clearly: 'Do unto me as you would have done unto you.' And then sticks to that offer. So any programme willing to co-operate with Tit for Tat could do so in the secure knowledge that Tit for Tat would never betray first. They could co-operate, and both win. Over all of its encounters with other strategies, then, Tit for Tat came out ahead.

This is very much a field of on-going research, and the scientists involved are the first to say that the prisoner's dilemma is only a model of human interactions. But it is developing into an explanation and predictor of a great deal of interactive behaviour. Dr John R. Hauser, professor of management science at the Massachusetts Institute of Technology, has found that it fits many situations in business and economics and it is now being used to investigate aspects of marketing, especially how competitors get into costly promotion wars and how to get out of them. To these working applications I would add my observation of its applicability to love and family relations, as I will explain in Chapters 8 and 9.

It is easy to see Tit for Tat as a well-adjusted little person. First, she is 'nice': she never initiates aggression or competition, always being willing to start off co-operating for mutual benefit.

Second, however, she is no submissive wimp, but a good example of self-respecting assertion, willing to retaliate in kind if attacked. Third, she harbours no grudges: as soon as you are willing to co-operate with her again, she is willing to resume co-operation and will not initiate aggression, despite your unkind treatment of her. Implicit in all of this is her recognition that overall she will win most by being co-operative rather than competitive, that her strategy assures her of winning *as much as was possible* and that is a realistic definition of success.

If you are telling yourself that all of this co-operation stuff may apply to computer games but not out there in the jungle of daily life, think again. A large body of research, gathered over more than thirty years, shows that co-operation works better than competition for humans, too. As long ago as 1954 sociologist Peter Blau of Columbia University compared competition and co-operation in the workings of an employment agency and found that co-operative staff filled more vacancies than did competitive staff. Psychologist Robert Helmreich at the University of Texas found that scientists who scored low on competitiveness were more likely to do research that was cited by other scientists (a practical index of scientific success). He repeated the study, with academic psychologists, and found the same result, so he extended his research to business people (using salary as an indicator of success) and undergraduate students (using grade-point averages as the indicator of success). In both groups he found the same result; that's right, business people who scored low on competition tended to have higher salaries. In 1985 he conducted three more studies, on fifth and sixth grade pupils, on airline pilots, and on airline reservation agents. The results in all three groups were exactly the same.

Many other researchers have studied the effects of competition versus co-operation in educational settings. In a review of 122 such studies, from 1924 to 1981, Professors David and Roger Johnson at the University of Minnesota found that in 65 cases co-operation did better than competition, in only eight had competition done better than co-operation, while in 36 there was no significant difference. In comparing co-operative with independent work, the Johnsons found that co-operation led to higher achievement levels in 108 cases, while independent work did better in only six cases, and there were no significant differences in 42 cases. As a result of their own research, the Johnsons have concluded that the discussion process in co-operative groups promotes the discovery and development of higher quality thinking strategies for learning than does the individual reasoning found in competitive or individualistic learning situations.

In the light of such consistent trends in such a large body of research on people in such a diverse range of settings, it really is time we buried the myth that competition brings out the best in people. It simply doesn't, unless you are looking at one of those unusual zero-sum game situations. Otherwise, co-operation works better and, given that most of life is a non-zero-sum game, the emphasis in our educational system should be on teaching co-operation, with competition as the less frequently used option when you are facing a genuinely zero-sum game (like football or netball). Co-operation can be taught effectively in school and I am pleased to report more teachers are doing that.

Despite the tenacity of the myths around competition, it is not as popular as you might expect, probably because it engenders anxiety and hostility, both of which are unpleasant. Many people who say they enjoy competing have had little experience of co-operation. When they do get to try out co-operation for themselves, they change their minds and, in 1984, the Johnsons cited no less than seven studies that showed that people who had tried both preferred co-operative to competitive situations. In 1986 marketing students at the Broadmeadows TAFE College in New South Wales, Australia, studied the attitudes of some 3,086 children towards playing sport. Most of the children considered fun to be the most important reason for playing sport, and they also valued being with their friends and gaining a sense of personal achievement. They did not consider beating their opponents as important and felt their coaches tended to adopt unnecessarily hard-line attitudes. They nearly all felt that rules and equipment should be modified to increase fun and enjoyment. I wonder how many adult administrators and coaches of children's sport will pay any attention to the kids' preferences, and what that shows about the adults' real motivation for being involved?

The compulsive aggressor

I think that aggressive, competitive people are like compulsive gamblers. Let me explain. Typically, compulsive gamblers had what they perceived as a big win at an impressionable stage of their lives. As a result, they come to believe they are *destined* to win and losses are interpreted as aberrations. In fact, they are overall losers, often paying a huge price in terms of the effects of their compulsions on careers, relationships and health. But their misguided belief is buoyed up by the occasional win, which is seen as how things ought to be, while the losses are misinterpreted as the exceptions. In fact, the evidence is clear enough, if only they would look at it realistically, that their wins are few and their losses are many.

A similar process seems to apply to simple-minded competitors. Starting out with a competitive approach they may win some initial victories. Adopting an aggressive style, they will scare some of the people some of the time, and win again. But quickly others recognize them for the bullies they are, and fight back and offer little support or assistance. Their assertive opponents will stand up to them and prevent any further easy wins, like Tit for Tat does. Their aggressive opponents will compete back, escalating the conflict, and sometimes inflicting losses. Increasingly the simple-minded competitor's energy and resources will have to be devoted to defence, and his real success rate is dropping. Misled by our culture's belief in simple-minded competition, he will misinterpret his losses as being due to not fighting hard enough and escalate even further. Encouraged by the occasional wins, he thinks that's the way things ought to be and does not realise that he is *not* winning as much as is possible. He is not a realistic success, even if he beats some other people some of the time.

The first trap of simple-minded competition is that it restricts your inter-personal style, locking you into competition without ever considering the possible advantages of co-operation, and so it reduces your real success rate below what it might have been.

No. 1 tip for success Discriminate! Ask yourself, is this a zero-sum game or a non-zero-sum game? Do I start by competing or co-operating?

And take a little time to think about it. Chances are that many of the situations you have taken as zero-sum games, believing someone must lose in order for you to win, are in fact non-zero-sum games where everyone could win, with a bit of creative problem-solving (see Chapter 5). Traditionally they may have been approached competitively, like our industrial relations, but that tradition results from unimaginative and antiquated thinking rather than a realistic consideration of the possibilities. There are surprisingly few real zero-sum game situations, and they are often clearly signposted by a stated and inflexible set of rules that require a zero sum of outcomes, like the rules for competitive sports. To maximise *your*

success rate, discriminate carefully and be flexible: willing to
co-operate when that will be mutually beneficial, and willing to compete when there really can be only one winner. Then you will be
winning *as much as possible*, and that is a realistic success.

The second trap of simple-minded competition is that you
adopt external criteria for success, forever comparing yourself with
others with the inevitable result of finding someone who beats you.
Then you will see yourself as failing, when realistically you may
have succeeded.

No. 2 tip for success   Win by making everybody a winner!

Whenever you have recognized a situation as a non-zero-sum game,
initiate co-operation by asking yourself, 'How can we all win here?'
Creative problem-solving is the process for finding win-win solutions (Chapter 5 again). Signal clearly to the others involved your
willingness to co-operate, by setting win-win goals. If you meet a
competitive, aggressive approach, respond assertively, like Tit for
Tat, but preferably a little softer so as to reduce the risk of
unnecessary escalation. Signal your willingness to co-operate
again, and always meet co-operative approaches with further
co-operation. If sadly you strike someone who is so misguided and
inflexible that he can only approach you aggressively and competitively, then assertively stick to your guns and match him blow for
blow. Neither of you will win as much as you might have, but you
will lose no more than is absolutely necessary, and you will know
that over all of your dealings you are winning more than this sim-
pleton will. The key to this approach is not to envy other peoples'
wins, especially those they gain by co-operating with you. Remind
yourself that, by co-operating whenever it is appropriate and possible, you are winning as much as you can and you cannot realistically be more successful than that. Envying others, comparing your
wins with theirs, may be the inevitable outcome of the competitive
approach popular in our culture, but it will cheat you of success, as I
will explain in the next chapter (and rob you of motivation, as I will
explain in Chapter 6).

3 | THE TRUTH ABOUT SUCCESS

> **success** 1. the favourable or prosperous termination of attempts or endeavours. 2. the gaining of wealth, position, or the like. 3. a successful performance or achievement. 4. a thing or a person that is successful. (*The Macquarie Dictionary*)

You will notice the dictionary is no fool; no mention in that lot about beating other people. Although that could be the 'favourable outcome' of your 'attempts or endeavours' at some competition — a genuine zero-sum game — it is not the *essence* of success, because it will only apply to those comparatively infrequent zero-sum situations, and not to the non-zero-sum majority of your activities. So, if success is not just winning by beating others, if it is not restricted to the occasional world champion, what is it? How do you decide when you have been successful?

Bob's Definition of Success

A real success is the person who performs at or close to the best of her or his ability, most of the time, in all of the important areas of his or her life. She or he will be as successful as his or her inherited potential, past experiences and present circumstances permit, in the careers of her or his choice, in intimate and social relationships, and in the recreations of his or her choice. She or he is making the realistic best of what he or she got in the lottery of life.

There is a number of key components in my definition and, to convince you that it should be your definition, I want to spell out each of them.

Be your own yardstick

First you will notice that, in my definition, your criteria for success are internal. Instead of comparing yourself — your performance, achievements, possessions, appearance — with others, you now compare yourself with **you**, with what **you** are capable of. If you are at or close to what you are capable of, then you are as successful as you can realistically expect to be. It is irrelevant, meaningless, and misleading to compare yourself with someone else, because she did not inherit your genes, has not had your life experiences, and does not inhabit your life situation. You may do something better than he does — you may beat him — because you fluked better genes for that activity or you were lucky enough to have parents who taught you how to do it well. You may do better than she without even trying much, without giving anything like the performance you are capable of. So, what's successful about being lucky or lazy?

The converse is equally true. He may do better than you — he may beat you — for reasons over which neither of you had any real control and which do not meaningfully reflect credit or shame on either of you. Comparing yourself with others will cheat you of some realistic successes, when in fact you have done as well as you could, and could lead you into wasting effort or distorting your life, trying to improve a performance that is already your realistic best.

No. 3 tip for success   Set realistic goals!

Taking into account the three broad factors I have outlined — your genetically inherited ability for the task in question, your relevant experiences up until now, and your relevant life circumstances at present — set realistic goals for yourself, adopt realistic standards for your performance. This is likely to take some thought for any important areas of your life. You probably won't have hard measures of your inherited ability. If it's important, you can get such estimates through testing by a qualified psychologist, at least as far as many skills and practical abilities are concerned. For other life areas, such as relationships, it is reasonable to assume you are unlikely to be genetically deficient in your abilities, even if you have not had much success lately. If you are in doubt about this, you could discuss your doubts with a qualified psychologist.

Look carefully at your relevant past experiences. Have there been events, or have you missed out on opportunities, that are likely to have influenced your present abilities? Look for the more subtle effects, as well as the obvious ones. If you attended a school where you were discouraged from studying mathematics, that could obviously be a contributor to your having trouble now with a statistics course. Less obviously, but just as certainly, having a father who criticised whenever you did anything could also be a contributor to your having trouble with your statistics course (or anything else). Don't do this review with the aim of finding *excuses* for a poor present performance, but rather to find possible *explanations*. It is a popular irrational belief that our present problems were caused by past events. Your lack of self-confidence may have *originated* in your father's sweeping criticisms, but its *maintenance* will be in your present thoughts and actions, which is great because you can change them, as I will be explaining. Look for relevant past experiences to set realistic goals for now — 'I don't expect to be a great skier if I have never had any lessons before' — and to identify possibilities for improvement — 'Now I have started skiing I can get a lesson each morning and practise each afternoon.'

Finally, look carefully at your present life circumstances, again for both the obvious and the subtle influences. You may be conducting your small business quite well, just staying afloat, during an economic recession over which you individually have little control. Less obviously, but just as certainly, coping with the stress of a failing marriage at home could be limiting your success at work. Again, I emphasize, this is not a search for excuses but for explanations, so that you adopt realistic goals and standards for now, and identify any possible goals for improvement.

No. 4 tip for success   Adopt internal criteria for success that are appropriate for you, then recognize your successes!

Adopting internal criteria for success means you are performing for an internal audience, that you are the most important judge in your life. It is good to receive praise or approval from others, no doubt about it. It is unpleasant to lose their approval or praise, no doubt about it. But it is not *essential* that you receive their praise or approval, for you to run a successful life. It *is* essential that you receive your own praise or approval when you have realistically earned it. This is the essence of a realistic self-esteem, which I believe underlies any successful life. When *you* think you have been successful most of the time, you feel motivated, as I will explain in Chapter 5. When *you* love yourself, meaning a realistic appreciation of your qualities and good points, then you can believe and accept love from others, as I will explain in Chapter 8.

You will have noted the important role I have ascribed to self-esteem in a successful life, but have you thought about the idea of self-esteem? The way many people talk about self-esteem you would think it was a substance, something you have a lot or a little of, that someone else can give you or take away. Take another look at the term: self-esteem. Esteeming yourself, seeing yourself as valuable (or not). In other words, self-esteem is not substance or a thing, but a set of behaviours. Every time you think or say or do something that is a value judgement of yourself, that *is* your self-esteem. You think: 'I did that reasonably well (or very badly).' Or you say, 'I can cook pretty well (or dreadfully).' Or you tackle something new because you believe you have a reasonable chance of succeeding (or you avoid trying it because you expect to fail). Those thoughts, words and actions *are* your self-esteem, because they are how you value yourself.

The trouble is, many of us have learned to make those value judgements unrealistically, usually unfairly negatively. Our past experiences included the parents, teachers or peers whose standards for approval were carrots on donkey sticks, always moving ahead of us, teasingly just out of reach. We were 'never quite good enough', we always 'should improve'. Gullibly, we accepted their unrealistic judgements. After all, they were only doing it 'for our good' (a fallacy they all sadly believed). Now, we make the same unrealistic judgements of ourselves, never recognizing what were realistic successes.

Well, too bad. So we had some bad luck in the past. Okay, recognize that fact in your review, as an explanation of why you now underrate yourself, but not as an excuse to keep doing it. Since your self-esteem is your self-judging behaviour, and you learned to do that unrealistically, now you can relearn it, more realistically. Having set realistic goals and realistic performance standards, recognize your achievements when you have them as the successes they are, and tell yourself: 'Hey, that's great! I did that as well as I could expect. Good for me!' And feel good about your successes.

You may want to add some self-encouragement, to continue improving, by setting your next, realistic goal, *but take the time now to recognize the success of achieving this one*. Then you are practising a realistic self-esteem, which is a key to real success and motivation.

No cats swallowing cream, please

My definition of success is not a recipe for smugness and complacency. I have emphasized that, in reviewing your past experiences and your present circumstances, you are not looking for excuses for a poor performance, but explanations for your present performance. In light of that review, and taking account of what you think your inherited potential for that area of your life could be, you may realistically decide your performance was not 'poor' at all, but reasonably close to your present realistic best. You probably only decided it was 'poor' by comparing it with someone else's performance, anyway.

On the other hand, you may realistically decide you *could* have done better, given your review. Fine, then pull your socks up! Work out a realistic and concrete strategy for improving and do it. You can feel content when you have achieved your personal, realistic best, given those three limiting factors. In the meantime, you may well have a number of current goals for improvement, each of which is getting its fair share of your time and energy, so that you are achieving a realistic rate of improvement. Don't be impatient. Some of the saddest people I see are the ones who have 'made it' by age 40, or even younger. They are successful at work, at least financially, although often becoming bored because 'the challenge has gone'. They have a big house, or two, a good-looking spouse and above-average children, although they may not be too close to any of them. By the criteria popular in our culture, they are successful, but they don't feel it. One of the main reasons for this is the limited nature of those criteria, typically emphasizing material success and external appearances, to the neglect or even detriment of other life goals.

My advice is, enjoy the tram ride because it's pretty boring sitting at the terminus. By this I mean take your time to enjoy the *process* of improving performances and achieving goals, rather than impatiently rushing towards 'perfection'. If you do happen to get to the terminus — you have achieved your current goals — and you have some spare time — you are not about to die — change trams and ride down a different route — find some new goals, probably broader than the ones you may have started adulthood with. The contentment that comes from my definition of success is not based solely on having swallowed the cream of your past successes, so that you now do nothing but sit in the sun, purring and indolent, although that can be a part of it. My contentment comes from knowing that I have achieved a reasonable number of my past goals, that I am doing reasonably well at achieving my present ones, and that I have plenty of new ones I would like to set, when I find myself with some spare time and energy. I am alive and living, successfully.

What *is* my personal best?

Good question. If you are going to recognize as a success the achievement of your personal best, given the influences of your genes, your past and present circumstances, how do you *know* when you have achieved that personal best? Easy: when you have devoted a reasonable amount of your time, energy and resources to that activity, then you are automatically and inevitably doing your realistic best. To do better (assuming that was possible), you would have to devote an unreasonable amount of your time, energy or resources to that activity and that will block you from achieving another key element in my definition of success, a balanced life.

Go back to my definition and you will see it has the goal of a balanced life built in: to be successful, you will be at or close to your personal best in your chosen career *and* intimate and social relationships *and* recreations. That's my thumbnail sketch of a balanced life and I see it as a crucial part of realistic success.

No. 5 tip for success   Plan and run a balanced lifestyle

When I was a kid going to see a circus, I used to marvel at the skills of some circus stars, some of whom looked no older than I. Gosh, they must be clever. Fancy being able to balance/climb/juggle/or whatever like that. Then I began to realize that the main ingredient of those performances was endless practice. You needed enough innate ability, and someone to show you the tricks of the trade, but given those all it took to be a 'star' was buckets of rehearsal and practice. In the glare of the lights with the circus band playing (they had live ones in those days) and the shiny costume and the shinier smile, it even looked like fun. Well, the people who choose that career may tell you it beats other routine jobs, but it has its own routine and repetition, and the repetition is necessary to achieve that star level of performance.

Since those days I have met enough 'stars' from all walks of life to realize there is a general principle involved. Some of us do well at some things because we fluked a natural ability for them. Some of us do well because we are lucky enough to have had good learning opportunities. Some of us do well because we are willing to practise, to build on our ability and learning. But many of the 'stars' excel at one activity because it is practically all they do. They are monomanically obsessed with the goal of being a 'star' at that activity — a business, a skill, a sport, a hobby — to the point that it occupies an unreasonable amount of their time and resources, to the neglect and damage of other parts of their lives.

And that's the point. I am not proposing a balanced lifestyle as a key part of realistic success for a philosophical, moral or religious reason; my argument is much more practical than that. My observation is that it is the people leading balanced lifestyles who are more likely to be consistently successful in all of the components of that lifestyle. Sure, you can be a 'star' in one part of your life by letting it hog your time. Bury yourself in it, and there you are, the richest person on your street, or the greatest lover or the most devoted mother. You may also be divorced or lonely, burnt out or a drunk, or last year's fading memory, but you were the champ . . . for a little while. My definition of success is more durable than that.

The successful balancing act

A balanced lifestyle is one that achieves three goals:

- You keep up with the essential tasks at work and at home
- You gain both pleasure and achievement from your activities
- You avoid unnecessary stress, to yourself and to your important relationships.

Keeping up with the essential tasks at work includes doing them reasonably well, achieving realistic goals for career development and promotion, perhaps mastering new work skills. It means you do not fall significantly behind, *providing the demands of your job are reasonable*, and that's an important proviso. Sadly, some jobs and some employers do put unreasonable demands on their workers. If that happens to you, and you are serious about being a realistic success, you will need to refuse the unreasonable demands assertively. I realize that's easy for me to suggest and hard for you to do, and that it may cost you a job if you are dealing with a very unreasonable employer, but I can only tell you what I think is true about being a realistic success.

What's successful about earning a high salary if earning it costs you your health, your well-being, your marriage, or your relationship with your kids? Beware of 'temporarily putting up with it', while you pay off the second mortgage or achieve some similar financial goal. I have seen plenty of people in therapy who thought they could put up with an essentially unbearable job for 'just a couple of years'. Urged on by their financial goal, they ignore or deny the warning signs of what this is costing them, until the total collapse of their health, their well-being, their marriage or family. Don't wait for the roof to fall in: if your job puts unreasonable demands on you, you can first try to improve it but, if it cannot be improved, get out of it, if you want to be a real success.

Keeping up with the essential tasks at home includes the chores of daily living, the repairs and maintenance on your dwelling, perhaps extending or improving it. It means not allowing your home or belongings to fall into unacceptable disrepair or dishevelment, *providing these demands are also reasonable*, and again that's an important proviso. Homes are for living in, not looking at. Don't be fooled by the glossy photos in *Home Beautiful*: you should see how much preparation goes into setting them up. The people most vulnerable to unreasonable domestic demands, often self-inflicted, are women who have chosen dual careers, a paid job outside home and still primary home-maker. If you (and your spouse) have decided you will work outside full-time, then recognize that means using some of your earnings to buy some domestic help, or you will wind up too exhausted even to notice how imbalanced your life has become. In between visits from your domestic helper, set realistic standards for home tidiness and cleanliness. If that means you have to scuttle around a bit before visitors arrive, welcome to the club.

We moved into our new home a few years ago and discovered, as any home-owner will recognize, an endless list of chores for completion, improvement or just plain upkeep. One sunny Sunday I was clambering around the roof, while my wife, Laurel, was down the front planting some trees. As I swung down from the roof I saw inside, glued to the TV, our son, Erin, heir-apparent to the family mortgage. 'What's this?' I thought, 'Why is he watching TV on a lovely sunny day when he should be out enjoying himself?' The answer was obvious: Dad was on the roof and Mum was digging in the garden (he was three then, and not really able to join in such activities) so what else could he do but watch TV? We had fallen into the easy trap of filling our spare time with chores. It is an easy trap to fall into. Those chores are such a *plausible* call on your time. 'Must get this done this weekend.' And there you are, leading an imbalanced lifestyle, succeeding at your chores and flopping at other equally important parts of your life.

A laugh and a chore a day keep the blues away

A balanced lifestyle gives you both pleasure and achievement: humans need both, to feel good and to feel good about themselves. All work and no play may make Jack a dull (and depressed) boy, but all play and no work will make Jill a worthless (and depressed) girl. I have seen examples of both kinds of imbalance, and even more depressed are the people getting neither pleasure nor achievement from their activities.

Pleasure means enjoyment, fun, a good laugh. If you are lucky, you will get some of this from your work, but most of us need to get our main supply from our recreation. Recreation is any activity that refreshes and relaxes you, so you can understand why it is an important component of both a healthy lifestyle and of successful stress-management. Given that, it is surprising how much it is often neglected. Recreation suffers because of our Protestant work ethic: since you don't get paid for it, it can't be really important. It's what you do in your spare time with your spare cash which means, since many of us have little of either, it often doesn't get done at all. That's very unfortunate because recreation has many possible contributions to make to being a realistic success. In Chapter 7 I will outline how to build good recreational habits, as part of your successful lifestyle. For now, make sure you have allowed sufficient time for fun in your life.

Achievement means the sense of having done something worthwhile and of having done it reasonably well. It may not be much fun, but it gives you a sense of purpose and makes an essential contribution to your self-esteem. Ideally most of us would be getting our achievement from our work, but poor job design has meant that has not always been the case and two trends are making it even less likely. First, the increasing applications of automation and computerization often result in the work left for humans to do being trivial and boring, and there is little sign of the engineers involved being aware of their impact on humans rather than machines. Incidentally, don't kid yourself that high tech is automatically the best path to improved productivity.

Second, the same changes to work design mean the supply of paid work is shrinking, at least when compared to the growing number of people looking for it. As a community, we have really not come to grips with this fact yet, and we are still dithering around talking about job creation and youth training schemes (to help them apply for jobs that will never exist). The pioneering days of the ever-expanding frontier are over, folks, and I doubt if Buck Rogers and moon colonies are going to bring them back. The unquestioned belief that growth is desirable — for example, that it will create all the new jobs needed to employ all the new workers — has fallen flat on its face in front of the fact that our planet is a finite resource, that it cannot support an infinitely growing population, that it cannot provide infinite raw resources, nor cope with infinitely increasing waste and pollution. In some areas more growth will be desirable and helpful; in others we will need a steady state or even reduction. I would not regard us as a very successful species if we consume and pollute ourselves into extinction and these are no longer idle threats.

As a part of the considerable revisions of attitude implied by all of this, we will have to rethink 'job' and 'work'. There simply will not be enough jobs or work to go around, as long as we define a job as a five-day week, or work as paid activity. Paid work may need to be shared around in smaller chunks and therefore will be less available as your source of achievement. This means we need to recognize the already existing potential of recreation as a source of achievement, as well as of fun. Right now you can be planning to obtain the achievement necessary to feel successful by choosing recreations that allow you to master new skills and new knowledge, to improve through practice and application, to be your personal best. Then you need only polish that off by accepting that this is worthwhile, because of its contribution to your health, your well-being, your self-esteem, and your relationships, even if you don't get paid for it.

Keeping the price reasonable

Any activity will cost you some of your time, some of your energy and some of your resources, and will therefore reduce your capacity to take part in any other activity. Running a balanced lifestyle means continual cost-benefit analyses: what is it costing me to be involved in this activity versus what am I getting out of it? When the cost outweighs the benefit, it's time to spend less on that activity. The third goal of your balanced lifestyle is to be achieving the first two — doing the essential tasks at work and home, gaining both pleasure and achievement — without imposing unnecessary stress on yourself or your important relationships.

Stress is a normal and inevitable part of being alive, and moderate levels of stress enhance your health, well-being and performance. Unnecessary stress is the overload that reduces your health, well-being and performance, so obviously has no part in being a realistic success. The symptoms of high stress can occur in all three areas above: if you have chronic or frequent health problems, if you often feel anxious, tense, angry, frustrated or depressed, or if your performance is down, particularly because of difficulties in concentrating, remembering or managing time, then you should consider doing a proper stress-management programme as part of your successful lifestyle.

You can get a good estimate of whether or not you are having problems with stress by completing the test on page 36 which was developed by Professor Charles Spielberger, one of the authorities in this field. Have a go at it now; instructions for scoring are below it.

Your score on the second half of the test, the general stress self-evaluation scale, is the more important because it reflects how you usually feel. The first half, measuring how you feel at the time of doing the test, naturally obtains more variable results, although I have found people with bad stress problems will score high on both halves. My rule of thumb is that any score of 50 per cent or more suggests a stress problem that deserves some concrete attention.

Don't forget that my definition of a balanced life includes no unnecessary stress on your important relationships, as well as on yourself. Your important relationships depend on your present life situation. If you are still young enough to be living at home with your parents and maybe some brothers or sisters, then they are probably the significant people in your life, along with any boyfriend or girlfriend and other close friends. If you are further down the track, the significant people in your life may be a spouse and children, or perhaps a circle of adult friends. Humans are social animals and there is research that shows that having good friends (which can include your spouse or family) is associated with good health; conversely, lacking friends or having troubled relationships is associated with bad health.

So listen to the significant others in your life. You may be

THE STRESS SELF-ASSESSMENT INVENTORY

PRESENT STRESS SELF-EVALUATION SCALE

Read each statement and then circle the number that indicates how you feel right now, that is, at this moment. There are no right or wrong answers. Do not spend too much time on any one statement, but give the answer which seems to describe your present feelings best. Add up the eight numbers you have circled to obtain your score.

	NOT AT ALL	SOMEWHAT	MODERATELY	VERY MUCH
I feel calm.	4	3	2	1
I am tense.	1	2	3	4
I feel upset.	1	2	3	4
I feel frightened.	1	2	3	4
I feel nervous.	1	2	3	4
I am relaxed.	4	3	2	1
I am worried.	1	2	3	4
I feel confused.	1	2	3	4

GENERAL STRESS SELF-EVALUATION SCALE

Read each statement and then circle the appropriate number that indicates how you generally feel. There are no right or wrong answers. Do not spend too much time on any one statement, but give the answer which seems to describe how you generally feel. Add up the eight numbers you have circled to obtain your score.

	ALMOST NEVER	SOMETIMES	OFTEN	ALMOST ALWAYS
I feel nervous and restless.	1	2	3	4
I feel satisfied with myself.	4	3	2	1
I feel that difficulties are piling up so that I cannot overcome them.	1	2	3	4
I feel like a failure.	1	2	3	4
I have disturbing thoughts.	1	2	3	4
I lack self-confidence.	1	2	3	4
I feel secure	4	3	2	1
I worry too much over something that really does not matter.	1	2	3	4

You can compare your score with the general population in this table. For example, if your score is on or above 50 per cent, you are more stressed than 50 per cent of men or women; if your score is on or above 75 per cent, you are more stressed than 75 per cent of men or women. A man with a present stress score of, say, 18 is experiencing more emotional stress now than than 75 per cent of men. A woman with a general stress score of, say, 22 generally experiences more stress than 75 per cent of women.

PERCENTAGE RANKS FOR PRESENT AND GENERAL STRESS SCORES

PER CENT OF POPULATION	PRESENT STRESS		GENERAL STRESS	
	MALES	FEMALES	MALES	FEMALES
95	21	25	23	25
75	17	17	18	20
50	14	15	15	16
25	12	12	13	13
5	10	10	10	10

coping fine, but how is your lifestyle affecting them? Earlier I described how destructive on marriages and families the Type A Behaviour Pattern can be, but your behaviour doesn't have to be that extreme to be causing stress to those around you. In Chapters 8 and 9 I will be emphasizing the role of good listening in making successful relationships but for now just listen to any complaints they may have about your availability to them — or lack of it — and your mood when you are available. If you accept my definition of success as including successful relationships, you may need to rearrange some of your lifestyle to be better available to the significant people in your life, in terms of both quantity and quality of time.

Designing a balanced lifestyle

Most of us drift into a lifestyle, without much deliberate thought or planning. You may only notice the pattern you have developed when it is not working, and even then you may only be aware of symptoms such as your spouse complaining that you are never around or your body complaining that it does not get enough rest or recreation. Different lifestyles suit different people and I am not going to suggest one plan that everybody should rigidly follow. But I will outline a process you can use to plan or revise your lifestyle, to achieve the balance you need to be realistically successful.

Step 1   Set your current goals

Take some paper and a pen, and write the headings below on it. Under each heading write your current goals in that area. You may have a long-term goal, although that is less necessary than many people believe, but you probably need a medium-term goal which in turn prompts some short-term goals. For example, under *Career* you may have a long-term goal of becoming departmental manager at work; the medium-term goal in that direction is to increase your sales by 30 per cent, and that implies short-term goals of finding some new potential customers and improving your sales skills. Or under *Family* you may have a long-term goal of staying happily married; the medium-term goal in that direction is to increase your common interests, especially as a couple, and that implies short-term goals of finding some potential shared activities and trying them out together. If you find you don't have any goals for an area, that probably means you have been neglecting it! Here are the headings I suggest you use.

Career   This probably means your paid job, unless you are currently working mostly as a home-maker, which is an important job, even if not paid. But it could mean unpaid work, such as volunteer or charity work.

Family   This includes your relationships and activities with your spouse, children, parents, brothers and sisters, and so on, as are applicable to you.

Friends   These are people you share recreation and relaxation with, and on whom you may occasionally lean for some support.

Learning/education   These are activities aimed at giving you new skills, knowledge or qualifications, which you may intend to use in your career, home or recreations.

Recreation   This is what you do to refresh and relax yourself; sharing recreation with your spouse, family, special friend or friends contributes to the maintenance of those relationships, as well. You can get ideas for possible goals from Chapters 7, 8 and 9.

Health   These are activities that improve and protect your health, most importantly nutrition, drinking habits, smoking habits, exercise and stress-management.

Personal development   These are activities aimed at helping you to grow personally, usually less directly task-oriented than those in Learning/education. For example, you may decide to improve your assertion skills, or take part in a prayer group at your church.

Others   This includes chores, both regular and irregular, like mowing the lawns or cleaning out the cupboards, but is not restricted to such mundane activities. One of the principles of effective time-management is to expect the unexpected, the unforeseen or unusual tasks that do crop up, however occasionally. If you have already committed all your available time, then you have no elasticity when one of these unexpected problems arises. You either cannot deal with it or something else you had planned to do gets dropped, to fit in this new problem, and there you are falling behind again. The practical point to this is to plan some unallocated time regularly. Then, when the unexpected crops up, you have some flexibility to fit it in.

Goal-setting is a skill in itself, and one that plays a crucial role in motivation. So I will explain it in detail in Chapter 7. If you have not had much practice at setting goals, you will find it helpful to do that chapter before completing this exercise.

Step 2   Set your current priorities

Within each area, rank the short-term goals in order of importance and accessibility. Both criteria are important; there's little point giving No. 1 priority to a goal that may be important, but is not available to you for now. You are asking yourself, 'Of these goals, which are the important ones I can tackle now?' Less important or less accessible goals can wait. Notice that you rank these priorities *within* each life area, *not* across areas. Your balanced lifestyle will have you attending to all of these areas, so there is no need to put the areas themselves in order of priority.

Step 3   Get a picture of your present lifestyle

Keep a record of how you currently spend your time. You will need to do this for at least one typical week, so that you include both weekdays and weekends. You may need to look at a longer timespan, perhaps referring to your diary or calendar, to get a reason-ably accurate estimate, including infrequent but regular calls on your time. You can use a form like the one opposite.

Step 4 Plan a more balanced lifestyle

Put your list of current priorities alongside your record of your current lifestyle and ask yourself: Which of my current short-term goals am I neglecting? Have I allowed one or two goals to eat up an unreasonable amount of my time, to the neglect of other goals? What changes do I need to make to achieve a more balanced life-style? When you have identified these, plan them and implement them. Lip service to success is no success at all.

Step 5 Review your lifestyle regularly

From time to time, check to see that you have not allowed yourself to drift into an imbalanced, unsuccessful lifestyle. You will achieve some of your short-term and medium-term goals, and they may need to be replaced. Occasionally you may decide a long-term goal should change, as your life situation changes, and as you yourself change. A handy checklist is the Four Rs: are you looking after your Rewards (both fun and achievement), your Relationships, your Recreation, and your Relaxation?

WEEKLY ACTIVITY SCHEDULE

HOUR	MONDAY	TUESDAY	WEDNESDAY	THURSDAY	FRIDAY	SATURDAY	SUNDAY
7/9							
9/10							
10/11							
11/12							
12/1							
1/2							
2/3							
3/4							
4/5							
5/6							
6/7							
7/8							
8/12							

4 | THE SKILLS FOR SUCCESS: COMMUNICATION AND CONFLICT RESOLUTION

To achieve your personal best, given the limits of your genes, your experiences and your present circumstances, you will need to be a skilful performer. An obviously necessary set of skills will be those required for the tasks in your life, in both work and recreation. I have neither the knowledge nor the space to cover even a sample of such skills, and, in any case, information about task-related skills is usually readily available. Use it. When you make a realistic appraisal of your performance on a particular task, you may decide you could expect to improve. Then get hold of the relevant information or training. Take the time necessary, but consonant with your balanced lifestyle, and you will be on the way to your personal best.

My topic for this and the next chapter is not skills related to any particular task, but rather skills for being successful at many tasks, in most if not all areas of your life. These are the basic interpersonal skills. How often have you seen someone whose outstanding skill at a particular task was largely negated by his inability to share that skill, or to work with the people around him? You may be great at your task but, if you upset the woman who supplies your raw materials or you offend the man who takes away the finished products or you alienate your superiors or your staff, then *your* final performance will suffer. Sure, you can blame all those others for 'letting you down' or 'not caring', but the truth would be that you did not approach the *whole* of your task with as much skill as you might have.

I have emphasized the need for you to be flexible, to be willing to compete or co-operate, depending on the circumstances, if you want to achieve your maximum possible success rate. It's likely you have been introduced to the ideas of successful competition; they are certainly flogged to death by sports coaches and pop psychology seminar speakers. But what do you know about the skills of successful co-operation? I have found that few people have had the chance to learn those. In this chapter I will introduce the skills for successful communication and conflict resolution, the skills that focus on the emotional side of interactions. In the next chapter I will introduce assertion and problem-solving, the skills that focus on the practical side of interactions although, as you will see, they are not exclusive of each other. In later chapters I will frequently suggest where you might use these skills to achieve success and build motivation.

Skilful communication

Communication is the medium through which human relationships are conducted. Poor communication means poor relationships with poor results for those within them. Dr Robert Bolton, an American expert in the field of interpersonal skills, says that 80 per cent of people who fail at work do so because they cannot relate well to others. The more you are promoted into supervisory or managerial positions because of your expertise at the job, the more your job changes to one of relating to people.

Most people do not communicate well since most of us have not had the chance to learn good communication skills. Humans are born able to cry, suckle and make a mess in nappies. We have to learn just about everything else. In the process of evolution, for the advantages of intelligence and flexibility of behaviour, we humans paid the price of having very little behaviour wired in genetically, compared to other species. So each human generation has to learn from scratch even basic behaviours that other animals simply inherit. This has given us the opportunity to develop new, sometimes cleverer behaviours, but it also carries the risk of learning ineffective behaviours. Obviously, most people spend some time trying to communicate in one way or another. One research study of people in various jobs found that they spent 70 per cent of their waking time in communication of one sort or another. People are often surprised when I suggest to them that they have a communication problem in their relationships, because they take good communication for granted.

The trouble is that you can say a lot to each other without really communicating much. This particularly applies to feelings. We have inherited much of the stiff-upper-lip approach to emotions: it's better not to have them, or at least not to show them (unless you are a woman, and therefore expected to have lots of them, but even then we'd rather you didn't show them). I have found repeatedly that attempts to deny or ignore feelings in any avenue of life not only don't work, they usually make things worse.

Feelings first

'What's this,' you may be thinking. 'I want to learn how to be a success and here we go, off into emotions. I don't want to waste time discussing my feelings.' Well, I am not going to suggest you convert your life into a continuous encounter group, but I am going to suggest that, if you want to deal successfully with other people, you must deal with any strong feelings first. Whether you like it or not, you will have feelings, you will express them, and other people will react to them. To pretend otherwise is to handicap yourself in your relationships, working or personal.

Of course, we communicate about more than feelings; we share facts, ideas, opinions, information, and the clear communication of these is also essential for successful relationships. It has been suggested that we are usually communicating in one or other of two modes. The first is the *emotional mode*, when you are trying to express your feelings or understand someone else's feelings. The second is the *problem-solving* mode, when you are sharing information and ideas, to solve problems. But your attempts to communicate these are so strongly influenced, possibly undermined or blocked completely, by the feelings in the situation that the strict rule of thumb for effective problem-solving is to deal with any feelings first. So, in this chapter I will introduce you to the skills for communicating in the emotional mode; the skills for communicating in the problem-solving mode are explained in the next chapter.

The basic communication skills

There are only three basic communication skills for the emotional mode, and it doesn't take long to learn them, although it may take some courage to begin using them and persistent practice to get good at them. Coupled with some sensible use of body language, which I have described below, these skills will enhance all your relationships. For each skill, I will describe both the dos and the don'ts; you will find there are few of the first, and lots of the second — there are many ways of not getting your message across or of discouraging someone from trying to get their message across to you. In practice, that means you should concentrate on learning the dos the good communication skills, because they are what you need to be able to remember on the spot. There are so many don'ts that you may wind up confused if you try to learn them off by heart. They are more useful as a checklist: if you are dissatisfied with the communication in a particular situation or relationship, read over the don'ts to spot which of the common communication errors you are making, then see if you can replace the error with a good communication skill next time. On the spot, you will find it easier if you concentrate just on using good communication rather than worrying about making mistakes.

Communication skill No. 1 Sharing feelings

Depending on the circumstances, from 60 to 90 per cent of your emotional impact on someone else is non-verbal; it is conveyed by your body language and the non-verbal cues in your voice, both of which we will consider in more detail later. Whether you like it or not, you give off vibes, and other people will respond to them. A few people, like a good actor, can fake or hide those vibes some of the time, but most of us can't, and trying to usually results in our sending confusing, mixed messages.

For example, your son has done something which makes you feel very angry but, to avoid conflict, you say to him, in a terse tone and through gritted teeth, 'OK, do it that way!' You have now put him in a bind: if he accepts your verbal message, he is ignoring the vibes, and will usually be troubled by that; if he responds to your vibes, he is ignoring your verbal message, and conflict may be more likely. Either way, he can't win, and neither does your relationship.

When you try to keep your feelings to yourself, you leave the other person no alternative but to mind-read. She will pick up your vibes, and then try to read your mind, to guess how you are feeling and why. However frequent mind-reading may be — everybody does it — it can be a dead trap. Research has found that the more strain there is in the situation or relationship, the more likely it is that mind-reading will be wrong, that the other person will guess you are feeling worse than you really are and that your bad feelings are directed towards her, when that may not be true. She then reacts to you in the light of her guesses, and the conflict is on. Your choice, then, is not 'Will I share my feelings with others?', because you will do that anyway, but 'Will I share my feelings accurately, or will I make other people read my mind, knowing they will probably get it wrong just when it would be helpful if they got it right?' For successful relationships, I recommend accurate communication.

Do share feelings clearly, promptly, and non-defensively. Telling people how you feel is called *levelling*. You can level under broadly two circumstances, depending on where your feelings are coming from. Firstly, if your feelings come from outside the relationship, level by announcing them. For example, you are feeling frustrated by a problem you are having balancing an account when a workmate comes over and asks you to have lunch with her. You feel angry because of the balance sheet, not because of her invitation but, if you don't level, she will pick up your vibes and could easily think you are angry at her. Protect your relationship by levelling: 'Thanks, Patricia, I'm fed up with trying to balance this account, but lunch would be good.' She now knows how you feel, but she knows it accurately, that your bad feelings have nothing to do with her or your relationship. Instead of being threatened by your obvious bad feelings, she may even be supportive: 'Yeah, it's a pain in the neck, that account. Have you checked last month's figures?'

Secondly, if your feelings come from inside the relationship — it is something the other person has done that is affecting you — level with an *I-language* statement, that is, 'When you do X the effect on me is Y and I feel Z.' For example, you play tennis each week with your friend, Peter. The last three weeks Peter has turned up late, so you have missed out on much of your game time. The next time it happens, you level: 'Peter, when you turn up late for tennis, I miss out on half of my fun and exercise, and I feel let down and frustrated.' If you don't level, Peter will pick up the vibes that you are feeling bad, but will have to guess why and may well get it wrong. By levelling *clearly*, you tell him exactly what is making you unhappy, and that's the first step in getting him to change it. By levelling *promptly*, as soon as he arrives late, you avoid stewing over and building up your bad feelings, and you don't give him the false impression that his behaviour is acceptable to you. By levelling *non-defensively*, speaking calmly if firmly and sticking to the X-Y-Z formula, you give yourself the best chance that he will not overreact (in the chapter on assertion I will outline how to handle the times when someone does overreact to your levelling). The X part of a levelling statement must be an observable behaviour, described as precisely as you can. For example, you might level: 'When you don't pass messages on promptly . . .' The other person knows exactly what he has done that you don't like. Your X should be something that Freddy Bloggs, an independent observer standing next to you, would be able to say, 'Yes, I saw (or heard) that happen.'

Don't make vague levelling statements, like: 'When you don't do your job . . .' The other person has to guess which part of his job you think he hasn't done.

Don't level with interpretations or judgements, like: 'When you can't be bothered passing on my messages . . .' Your interpretations and judgements of other people's behaviour are *your* responsibility, may or may not be correct, and are likely to block communication and increase conflict.

Don't over-generalize, like: 'When you *always* forget my messages . . .' or 'When you *never* pass on my messages . . .' It is rare for an over-generalization to be true and, even if it is, levelling with one invites the other person to look for the exception — 'I remembered to tell you last Friday' — and avoid your present concern.

Don't character-assassinate, like: 'You are a lazy and unreliable no-hoper . . .' Tell someone you think she has a faulty character or a deficient personality and you are most likely to receive a hostile response and no behaviour change. Tell someone how you feel about a particular part of her behaviour, and she may be willing to change it.

The **Y** part of a levelling statement should be a clear, brief description of the concrete effects of the other person's behaviour on you. Continuing our example, you might next say: 'My customers blame me for not returning their calls . . .' The other person is more likely to change his behaviour if he can see that it has concrete effects on you, than for other reasons. You are not justifying your feelings at this point — you don't have to, you're entitled to them. You are explaining to the other person that his behaviour has affected you materially, by costing you time or money, damaging your property, hurting you physically or emotionally, or interfering with your work.

Don't moralize, like: 'You ought to be more reliable . . .' Moralizing implies that your morals are superior to hers and that will block communication and lessen your influence.

Don't lecture, like: 'You should make a list of things that need to be done each night . . .' Lecturing implies that you are superior to the other person, and that will block communication and lessen your influence.

Don't order or threaten, like: 'You must pass on my messages promptly or you will be sacked . . .' Orders and threats only appear to work while the threat is present and large; even then, they again imply a superior-inferior relationship and create resentment, inviting hidden disobedience or retaliation.

Don't level on someone else's behalf, like: 'You are upsetting and offending the customers . . .' Other people can level for themselves, if they want to. You are actually belittling them, and their ability to speak up for themselves, when you do it for them.

Don't level on the wrong issue, like: 'You are making us look incompetent . . .' when your real concern is the bad impression your customers may get of you. Level on the wrong issue and the other person may give you the wrong behaviour change.

The **Z** part of your levelling statement should be a clear and accurate expression of your feelings, as personal as you think is appropriate for this relationship. Continuing our example again, you might say: '. . . and I feel very frustrated.' If the relationship was reasonably close and important to you, you might add the more personal information, '. . . and let down by you.' In a distant relationship, you might only want to say that you feel 'bad'. Try to be accurate about both the *flavour* and the *intensity* of the feeling.

Don't try to keep your feelings to yourself by omitting the Z part or not even levelling at all. As I have emphasized above, you will share your feelings, accurately or inaccurately. People are sometimes reluctant or embarrassed to level about their feelings, especially if they have not done much of it before. You can help yourself overcome these barriers by thinking: 'I expect to feel awkward about sharing my feelings openly when I haven't done that much before, but I won't die of feeling awkward and it is important to me to have successful relationships. So, work out what I want to say, and give it a try.'

Don't blame others for your feelings, by using statements, like: 'You make me frustrated.' Other people do not control and therefore are not responsible for your feelings. Their actions *influence* how you feel, but you finally control them, especially their intensity, by how you think and act in the situation.

Don't weaken your levelling, with modifiers, like: 'I feel a little frustrated' or 'sort of let down'. If you make the situation seem unimportant to you, that may be how the other person sees it too. People are usually tempted to weaken the feelings in their levelling statements for the same reasons they are reluctant to assert themselves generally, and I will deal with those reasons in Chapter 5.

Wrapping up levelling, then, you are going to say: 'When you don't pass on my messages promptly, my customers blame me for not returning their calls, and I feel very frustrated and let down by you.' A couple of other suggestions about levelling:

Don't make your levelling statements too long or complicated, like: 'When you don't pass on my messages promptly because you've rushed off to do your own thing and left things in a mess, my customers think I couldn't be bothered calling them back and then they take that out on me and I lose sales and I'm feeling really fed up about you letting me down like that.' Whew! If you want the other person to get your message, make it as easy as possible, not a memory competition. The times you are most likely to need to level is when you and others are upset, and you and they won't cope with complex messages. The communication skills work in difficult situations because they are simple and easy to follow. Stick to the formula.

Don't lash out, try to hurt back because you are feeling hurt, like: 'I thought you were my friend, but you can't be trusted to do anything right.' When someone hurts you, you can be tempted by the short-term goal of revenge, and it may give you some short-term satisfaction, but obviously at a cost to the relationship. If you want the relationship to work as well as possible, level when you feel hurt by something the other person did, and you give her the best chance of responding constructively.

Don't only level about bad feelings. If all or most of the feedback someone gets from you is negative, he will feel devalued by you and that blocks communication and lessens your influence. Use your communication skills to share good feelings, too, when it's appropriate, like: 'I really appreciate the way you have been passing on my messages so promptly since we talked about it.'

'But,' you may be thinking, 'what if she doesn't pass on my messages even if I level about it ten times. I still haven't solved the problem.' Quite right, you haven't. Remember, in this chapter we are dealing with the emotional mode of communication; problem-solving comes next. For example, it's quite common to follow a levelling statement with a request for change; I'll explain how to do that in the next chapter. Levelling is the skill for sending information about your feelings. Next we'll look at the skills for receiving that information but first I recommend you practise making some levelling statements.

Communication skill No. 2   Listening

Listening looks easy: point your ears in the direction of the other person and it should just happen. It doesn't. People spend a lot of time apparently listening; you will remember I reported earlier that people in a number of jobs spent 70 per cent of their waking time in communication of one sort or another. Only 30 per cent of that communication time was talking, while 45 per cent was listening. Yet many research studies have found that people generally do not really take in much of what they seemed to be listening to. When just information is being communicated, three-quarters of what is said is ignored, misunderstood, or soon forgotten. When feelings are being communicated, the real message may not even get across at all, either because it wasn't sent clearly or because the listener doesn't know how to receive it.

There is a world of difference between hearing and listening. Hearing is the physical and physiological process of a sound being received by the mechanisms in your ear and transmitted to your brain as nerve impulses. Hearing depends only on the sound being loud enough, the level of competing sounds being low enough, and your not being deaf. Sometimes you will hear sounds you do *not* want, like a distracting noise when you are trying to listen to some music, or a dangerously high level of noise from a machine digging up the road.

Listening is an active process, it is your interpretation and understanding of what you hear, or at least the parts you choose to attend to. The key components in active listening are attending, interpreting and understanding, and these are the make or break of successful listening.

Do attend actively to the other person. To strengthen listening skills, I suggest you pretend to be a tape recorder. This does not mean that your eyeballs go around in circles; it does mean that you should be able to play back to the other person what he just said to you, in his words, as though you were a tape recorder. I am not suggesting you repeat back everything anyone says to you, although occasionally repeating messages can be helpful, as I'll explain shortly. I am suggesting you set the goal of being able to play back what was said to you, if you wanted to. You will find that you need to listen carefully to be able to do a word-for-word playback, and that gets you attending actively.

Do show you are attending. Attending actively not only helps you receive the other person's message, it encourages the other person to communicate with you, which could be essential if she is uncertain about opening up to you. Much of your willingness to listen is expressed non-verbally, so make a conscious effort to use the body language of listening. *Face the other person*, and *lean towards her* a little, rather than away. *Keep a comfortable distance* between you, not too close and not too far away. In British culture, this is usually around one metre, but be aware of possible cross-cultural differences. Try to *keep reasonable eye contact*, around half of the time looking at the other person's eyes.

Don't interrupt, even if you have strong feelings on the topic. If you interrupt you are assuming you know what the other person is going to say, and you may be wrong. Even if you were right, interrupting shows the other person you are not willing even to let him have his say, and that usually escalates any conflict. If you have a habit of interrupting others, catch yourself, preferably before it happens, and tell yourself: 'Shut up! It's my turn to listen now. I am not necessarily agreeing, just showing my willingness to listen. I can always say my piece later. Now listen! What exactly is he saying?'

Don't monopolize the conversation by doing most or all of the talking. If you don't let other people get a word in, you won't hear what they have to say. If, like me, you tend to be a bit of a talker, try Montgomery's finger-in-mouth technique. To remind myself to keep quiet and let the other person say what she really wants to, especially when I am conducting a therapy session, I have found it helpful to stick a finger or a pen in my mouth. Try it; you'll find it's quite difficult to talk with something stuck in your mouth, and I find it reminds me to shut up and let the other person have her say. Some people find it difficult to cope with silences in the conversation because they feel awkward or impatient. But the other person may be silent because he is working out what he wants to say and he does not need to be interrupted by you; he will usually show this by looking away from you. If he is lost or stuck for words, he will usually show that by looking at you, and then you might helpfully say something. Otherwise, help yourself to cope with silences by thinking: 'It is not essential or even normal for someone to be speaking all of the time; silence is a normal part of conversations, while people are thinking; relax, and wait to hear what he wants to say.'

Don't hide behind the furniture or your body armour. If you put barriers, like large desks, between you and other people, they will respond to the distance you are keeping between you by communicating less. In our consulting rooms, we have lounge chairs and low, coffee tables for furniture, to create a relaxed atmosphere that supports communication. 'Body armour' refers to hiding behind your posture, usually by folding your arms and crossing your legs, and sitting rigidly inside your little anatomical fort. Try to adopt an open and relaxed posture.

Do interpret accurately and thoughtfully. We normally tend to interpret incoming messages in light of our own attitudes and expectations, and they can distort those messages considerably; we often see and hear what we expect, rather than what is really there. For effective communication, you need to hear what the other person really said, rather than what you expected her to say, so first try to receive her message accurately. The tape-recorder technique above is appropriate here. If you are ever not sure that you received a message correctly, check it by playing it back. Continuing our earlier example, the recipient of the levelling statement might check the accuracy of her listening by saying: 'You said that when I don't pass on your messages promptly, your customers blame you for not returning their calls and you are feeling frustrated about that. Is that right?' Many unnecessary disputes could be avoided if people just checked the accuracy of their listening first. You may find it difficult just to play back a levelling statement, without making any comment, if you don't agree with it. But remember you are not agreeing, just showing your willingness to listen. You can always level about how you see the situation later.

Having received the other person's message accurately, think about it, to see if there is more to it than may be immediately apparent. Beneath the apparent message, there may be a deeper one, that the other person has difficulty saying, or even recognizing himself. For example, your spouse may level to you that she doesn't come to your staff social functions because she thinks the food is nutritionally poor, but everything about how she levels suggests to you that nutrition is not the real issue. You may get the impression that she actually avoids the social functions because she feels shy with some of your workmates. Changing the food will do nothing to solve the real problem. Dr Bolton argues that fixing minor problems while not addressing the deeper issues is one of the major sources of inefficiency in organizations.

Do show your understanding. You will realize that you are guessing the other person's real concern at this stage, but you avoid the mistake of relying on this mind-reading if you *check your interpretation*, by reflecting it back. This involves paraphrasing — saying what you think the other person is really feeling, in your own words, and giving him the chance to correct you, if your guess is wrong. Continuing the example, you might reply: 'It sounds to me as if you are worried about more than the food in the canteen. Is there something else about mixing with my workmates that is putting you off?' If your guess was wrong, the other person will soon tell you; if you were right, he may now feel able to discuss his real concern with you; in either case, he gets the message that you are trying to understand him.

You will also notice that your reflection of his feelings included a question, inviting him to tell you more. This will work best if you *use open-ended questions*, questions that give the other person maximum freedom in how she answers. A closed-end question presumes you know the likely answer already, like: 'It sounds to me that you are not getting on with some of my friends. Is that right?' The other person can really only answer 'yes' or 'no', and may resent your presumption. The open-ended question, like 'Is there something else bothering you?' gives the other person an invitation to talk about her concerns as she sees them.

The most effective way to show your understanding is to validate the other person's levelling, and that I will explain next, but do take some time to practise your active listening skills.

Communication skill No. 3   Validating

To validate someone's levelling to you, you simply show that you accept what he has told you about his feelings as being true for him. Continuing our earlier example, the listener could validate by saying: 'Yes, I can see how you would be getting frustrated by that.' If you think about it, validating should be simple and easy, because it just boils down to believing what the other person has told you about her feelings. But many people find it difficult, because they confuse validating with giving in, or with seeing things the way the other person does, or with admitting they meant to make the other person feel like that. It's none of these; validating just means you accept what the other person told you about his feelings, because he told you.

Do validate clearly, promptly, and non-defensively. You won't always understand *why* the other person feels as she does because you are two different people, and it isn't necessary to be able to get completely into her shoes to be able to validate. The minimum necessary is to say, 'I understand that is *how* you feel', because that is what you have just heard her say. If it is true, you can show the deeper level of understanding by saying, 'I understand *why* you feel like that,' but don't say it if it isn't true. People can usually pick phony statements of understanding and they really block communication.

Don't refuse to validate because you would feel differently if you were in the other person's situation, like: 'Well, I wouldn't mind if a few customers complained.' You are listening to his feelings, not imagining yours.

Don't defend your actions when they have an effect you didn't intend, like: 'Well, I didn't think the customers would blame you.' If you didn't intend to make the other person feel bad, you don't have anything to defend. You will often find your impact on someone else is not what you intended and, as they react badly, there is a lot of pressure on you to be defensive. Don't. Make your real intention clear, if you want to, but still validate. For example, 'Yes, I can see you would feel frustrated about that. I didn't mean to cause trouble for you, but I can see that it would.'

Don't dodge the issue by picking up on something that is more important or interesting to you, like: 'That must be frustrating the customers,' or by avoiding the other person's real concern, like: 'Well, I suppose we always lose some sales.'

Don't tell the other person to be logical and therefore stop feeling bad, like: 'Well, I don't see what you're getting upset about, it doesn't hurt them if they have to wait a little longer to talk with you.' Despite the lip service paid to logic, as I mentioned earlier, humans do not usually think or act logically. Our feelings are plausible to the person having them, and that's what counts.

Don't reassure the other person and therefore expect them to stop feeling bad. If I had a dollar for every time one of my clients has been told to 'Stop worrying' or 'Cheer up' I could retire; if I had a dollar for every time simple reassurance has not helped, I could retire even sooner. Denying other people's feelings by telling them to be logical or by reassuring them often makes them feel worse because you are telling them it is wrong for them to be feeling bad in the first place, and that may make them reluctant to communicate further with you.

Don't bring up the past to defend your present actions, like: 'Well, you forgot to give me my messages last week.' If the other person did something in the past that affected you, you should have levelled then. Remember my earlier advice about not storing up bad feelings; level promptly. Now you should be dealing effectively with the present situation by validating the other person's feelings.

Body talk

Because I have been concentrating so far on what to say to share feelings effectively, you may have lost sight of the research finding I quoted earlier, that 60 to 90 per cent of your emotional impact on someone else is non-verbal. Your non-verbal communication skills will make more impact than what you say, so they deserve some systematic attention, too. In fact, I did outline the non-verbal components of good listening while describing that skill, because so much of listening is inevitably non-verbal. You may like to go back and refresh my suggestions there about body position, inter-personal distance, and eye contact. The last is very important, because where your eyes are looking has a big influence on the other person.

In a comfortable conversation, people have eye contact between 25 and 75 per cent of the time; 100 per cent eye contact is usually aggressive (unless you are passionately in love, which is really another form of aggression, anyway); zero eye contact is usually pretty offputting, too. If you are out of practice at levelling, then peering into someone else's eyes and saying, 'Look, when you did X the effect on me was Y and I felt Z,' *you* will feel uncomfortable. So what? No one ever died of feeling uncomfortable and, if you want good relationships with others, you will need to level effectively, including having reasonable eye contact. You can help yourself to cope with this discomfort by thinking: 'I expect to feel uncomfortable when I try to keep up eye contact while I level, but I can cope with feeling uncomfortable and it's not a good enough reason for me not to communicate well.'

As well as using your own body language to improve communication, you can try to read other people's body language, especially to help you interpret their messages correctly. **Do deliberately look for non-verbal clues**, including the *tone, volume and pace of speech*, apart from the words, and the other person's *facial expression, posture and gestures*.

Don't kid yourself about the accuracy of your interpretations of someone's body language. Despite the pop psychologists' confidence in their ability to read the exact meaning of every twitch of the body, their predictions run well beyond existing research, as pop psychologists often do. The exact meaning of a piece of body talk will depend on what else is happening at the time, especially what is being said, and on the psychological make-up and culture of the person. Body language gives clues, not guarantees, about the other person's feelings, and you should check these clues, as suggested above in the listening section.

Do look for contradictions within the total message, like when the person looks and sounds bad, but says, 'I'm okay.' She is really sending you two messages: 1 I feel bad, but 2 I don't want to accept that or I don't want to talk about it. You need to deal with both messages, which you can do by levelling on the contradiction: 'When you look and sound miserable but tell me you're okay, I don't know how you would like me to act, and I feel confused.' You might then invite her to level again, 'I don't want to stick my nose in, but is there something wrong?' Of course, you accept her right not to level with you if she doesn't want to.

Anger management

I began by saying that you must deal with the feelings in a situation first, if you want to go on to effective problem-solving. This is particularly true when someone is angry and in situations of conflict. If you don't deal with those strong feelings first, they will always interfere with your problem-solving, will often escalate, and can even take over from the original issue and prolong the conflict uselessly. Some conflict is inevitable in any human organization. It would probably be more peaceful if that wasn't so, but the fact is, if you put two people on the same planet, sooner or later they would tread on each other's toes, if only by accident.

In any case, some experts believe that conflict can have useful functions, as well as destructive ones. Being able to express anger and deal with conflicts openly and constructively within families seems to be associated with high self-esteem in the children and better love relationships amongst the adults. Within organizations, conflict can prevent stagnation, encourage the search for new solutions and developments, and foster better understanding, of yourself when you are obliged to explain your position, and of others when you listen to their positions. Useful conflict is likely to be *realistic conflict*: the clash of opposing wants, goals, solutions, values or interests. Realistic conflict can be managed by using good interpersonal skills. *Unrealistic conflict* results from ignorance, prejudice, tradition, poor organizational structures, aggressive competition, hostility and excessive anger. It can be prevented or at least controlled by using good interpersonal skills.

On the individual level, anger can serve useful functions as well as destructive ones. Anger, like all emotions, is a normal human response and attempting to deny or suppress it usually makes it worse, and can have a number of negative side-effects. Accepting your anger and expressing it openly and assertively can energize you, increase your motivation to tackle a problem, increase your feeling of being in control and capable, and ultimately increase your self-esteem. Expressing it aggressively has a destructive effect on your relationships, increases the level of conflict, and ultimately lowers your self-esteem.

So, anger and conflict are inevitable and normal, and both can have positive and negative effects. That's why I am talking about the *management* of anger and the *resolution* of conflicts, not about the elimination or suppression of either. First, what can you, as an individual, do about your own anger?

I discourage you from levelling with 'you-statements' in which you blame someone else for your feelings, like: 'You make me angry.' You-statements are simply wrong, because no one else can actually make you feel anything. Other people's actions can *influence* how you feel, but they do not *control* it. You finally determine how you are feeling, especially how intense those feelings are, by how you choose to think and act in the situation. If you choose to think in negative and defensive ways, and to act in aggressive or defensive ways, you can make yourself quite angry. But you did it to yourself; all the other person did was to provide the stimulus for you to overreact to. If you don't want to feel so angry, it's up to you to stop overreacting. So, the first step in anger management is to *accept that you are finally responsible for your level of arousal*.

This is difficult for some people, because they have made a lifetime habit of passing the buck for their bad feelings, encouraged by our culture's view of feelings as being controlled by factors outside the person. How often have you heard someone say some-thing like: 'She annoys me' or 'Going to the club relaxes me' or 'Losing that contract has really depressed me'? In our daily con-versations, we talk about our feelings as being caused by factors outside ourselves. In fact, a large body of research shows that this is not true. Humans think, and our thinking turns out to be a very important part of our total behaviour. It is not the external factors that finally determine how we feel, but how we think about those external factors. Excessive bad feelings of any sort, including anger, result from unrealistic and exaggerated thinking. The way to eliminate the excess is to make your thinking more realistic. The process for doing this we call *mental relaxation*. If anger is a per-sonal problem for you, I strongly suggest you buy a book on mental relaxation and spend some time and effort learning this skill.

The second step in anger-management is to *learn to track your level of arousal*, so that you can do something constructive before you get very angry. Once you are frothing at the mouth and leaping about, it's a bit difficult to think or act sensibly. Although I will later outline a procedure you can use even at the height of conflict, it's preferable not to let things escalate that far, because of the inherent waste of time and emotions. You will be more able to act constructively in a potential conflict situation if you take steps early to prevent your anger from becoming excessive. So teach yourself to be sensitive to the early warning signs that you are becoming angry. The common ones are an increase in muscle ten-sion, a change in your breathing, either faster or irregular, raising your voice, talking over other people, and the feelings of annoy-ance, frustration or anger. But observe yourself, and see if there are any other cues of rising anger that you can use to prompt you to do some anger management immediately. It can also be helpful to pinpoint situations that, from past experience, you think are likely to be provocative for you, and be consciously ready to use anger management skills when you enter those situations.

If you do find your arousal is rising and you are on the way to becoming angry, you can lower your arousal by using a *calming response*, based on a technique developed by Dr Charles Stroebel and his colleagues. This is a four-step procedure that only takes six seconds, so you can use it on the spot, without interrupting the flow of your activities. You can even use it during a conversation or discussion, because the only effect on the people you are talking with is to make you appear thoughtful, which won't hurt your image. The four steps are:

Step 1 Mentally detach from the situation and smile to yourself.

As soon as you can step back from the situation, even mentally, it will have less impact on you. Smiling to yourself, laughing at the situation, not only brings about that detachment but also introduces the calming effect of humour. You will often find there is a funny side to conflicts, including your own contribution, if you are willing to look for it. Do make sure you are smiling to yourself, inside your head, which you can usually feel as a relaxation of the muscles around your eyes. A big grin on your face could be taken as provocative by other people.

Step 2 Think to yourself: 'Clear head, calm body.'

This is a brief instruction to yourself: my mind will stay alert while I deal with this situation, but my body will relax. If you prefer to write your own calming self-instruction, do so, but keep it brief.

Step 3 Take in one, slow, deep breath.

Your mind reacts to your body's reactions. Researchers have found that panic-prone people can bring on a panic attack simply by breathing fast and shallow, and conversely can control a panic attack by deliberately slowing their breathing. Taking control of your breathing and making it slower and deeper will enhance your feeling of being in control.

Step 4 As you breathe out, relax your body.

Imagine a wave of relaxation, starting in your face and head, and flowing down through your neck and shoulders, and on down to your feet.

That's it. Reading it through for the first time, and the first few times you try it, it may seem a bit stilted and awkward. But, with enough practice, it can become your habitual way of responding to any provocative situation, helping you to keep your arousal at a reasonable level. You should do that practice before you really need the calming response; take a few minutes to imagine, as vividly as possible, past or potential provocative situations and, when you can imagine yourself becoming angry, imagine yourself using the calming response. This imagined rehearsal of new skills transfers very effectively to the real world, and I suggest you use it to strengthen your other skills, such as communication and assertion, as well.

Finally on the individual level, you should express your anger constructively, using the communication skills above. Don't kid yourself that others won't know you are angry or react to your anger; level, and give them the chance to react constructively. If you are in a conflict, use the assertion skills in the next chapter to stick up for your viewpoint, while respecting those of other people. If the conflict is over the preferred solution to a problem, stick to the problem-solving procedure described in the next chapter. When things are getting hot, don't tell everyone else what *they* ought to do; look at your own behaviour and see what *you* can do.

Conflict resolution

Above I have outlined the steps an individual can take to manage his anger and prevent it from interfering with fruitful discussions. Now I will outline the steps that two or more people, in a potential or actual conflict situation, can take to prevent or contain conflict. To have your best chance of using these ideas successfully, all of the people involved should know them, to be able to recognize a co-operative initiative when one occurs and to know how to respond in kind. So, share them around.

Again, *look for the early warning signs* of rising conflict. Ideally the first person to become upset should take the initiative to use the following procedures. In the real world some people won't do that. So, if it appears to you that someone else is getting angry but not doing anything constructive about it, you can initiate the following steps. Common cues to rising tempers are increasing volume and pace of speech, and people beginning to interrupt and talk over each other. It can also help to identify common trouble-spots: situations or issues that frequently lead to conflict. When one of these comes up, remind yourself to make a conscious effort to use the skills in this chapter. As with individual anger management, the earlier some constructive steps are taken, the better the chance of their being successful.

As soon as it becomes apparent that conflict is looming, *stop the action!* The upset person, or someone else if she doesn't take the initiative, acts like a movie director, and stops the scene. 'Hold it, I'm getting angry here (or, you look like you're getting angry); I would like to stop the discussion for a minute.' The discussion stops, and instead you focus on *how* you were talking, rather than *what* was being discussed. At this point, you have several choices:

 – *Can we pick up the discussion better, straight away?* This usually means making a conscious effort to get back to using communication, assertion, or problem-solving skills, whichever may be appropriate.

– *Should we start again?* If the discussion has gone off the track, well away from the original or intended topic, as often happens when feelings rise, you may benefit from beginning again, with a deliberate effort not to sidetrack.

– *Or am I (or are you) too upset to go on sensibly now?* If anger has reached the point where going on will only lead to further escalation, then there really is no point going on. Despite the occasional pop psychologist's recommendation that fights are good because they clear the air, in fact uncontrolled arguments are destructive of problem-solving, of relationships, and of self-esteem. For everyone's sake, including your own, refuse to squabble.

To stop an impending fight from developing any further, *take time out from the discussion.* 'I'm too upset (or you're too upset) for this discussion to go anywhere useful now. I would like to take half an hour to cool down. Agreed?' Notice that taking time out constructively, you *always make an appointment to return to the discussion.* Time out is not the passive aggressive response of just walking out, usually slamming the door behind you, which effectively says to everyone else that you don't think they're worth talking to. Time out is a constructive response that says, 'I do want to work out this problem with you, but not by fighting, so let's take time out to cool down.'

If time out is initiated, *use the time to cool down and work out a constructive approach to the issue.* It is an easy temptation to use the break to stew over your grievances and fan your anger, planning your next salvo to unleash as soon as the battle resumes. In the meantime, you will be making yourself feel worse and making conflict more likely when you do go back. Use the calming response to cool down and then plan a constructive approach to the issue in conflict. Plan, and rehearse in your imagination, how you can present this approach assertively when you go back.

Then try to stick to your plan, not rigidly nor regardless of what others have to say, but in preference to becoming angry again. If necessary, *recycle these steps* as often as you need to prevent unnecessary conflict, while you work towards a resolution of the issue, using the problem-solving procedure. If that takes longer than just bulldozing through a decision amidst mutual insults and accusations, it will nonetheless promote more successful relationships and develop a shared commitment to the final decision, thus building people's motivation to carry it through.

5 | THE SKILLS FOR SUCCESS: ASSERTION AND PROBLEM-SOLVING

In the previous chapter I outlined the two interpersonal skills that focus on the emotional side of interactions. Now I will introduce the two sets of skills that focus on the practical side of interactions, assertion and problem-solving. However, I repeat my earlier point that these skills are not exclusive of each other. In dealing with others successfully, you will slip from one skill to another as appropriate. Needless to say, that takes practice.

Assertion

Although I have listed assertion as an interpersonal skill, that is misleading and over-simple. Even considering it as a set of skills runs the risk of your seeing it as a trick bag of techniques for getting your own way, which is unfortunately how it is often presented. Assertion is an interpersonal *style*, it is (or should be) the usual manner of your relating to others. Although I will suggest assertive approaches to each of some common situations, they are just examples of being assertive. As you become more skilful at assertion you should easily be able to adopt an assertive approach to any situation. Assertion is important to my definition of success: you will recall that being co-operative does not mean being a wimp — you can stand up for yourself effectively when you are approached aggressively — but neither does it mean you are unnecessarily aggressive — you can co-operate for mutual benefit, whenever that is appropriate. Assertion is the human equivalent of the Tit for Tat programme, winning for you your best possible success rate in dealing with others.

There are basically three interpersonal styles: submission, aggression and assertion.

Being submissive means keeping your thoughts, opinions and feelings to yourself; not speaking up when you should; and allowing others to walk over you, to treat you unfairly or unkindly, and to rip you off. The usual motivation for being submissive is a fear of the judgements or reactions from other people if you did speak up. The submissive person fears feeling anxious when he speaks up and fears feeling bad if the other person reacts negatively, so he shuts up. Sometimes people are submissive because they confuse it with being polite. In any case, the submissive person finally gives himself a poor deal: he temporarily avoids the possible bad feelings from being assertive, but then usually pays a higher cost in terms of lost self-esteem, recognising how he has let himself down. In the process, he has also let someone take away some of his personal rights, and may set up a continuing pattern in which his rights will be violated again.

Aggression involves sticking up for yourself, asking for what you want, and refusing what you don't want, but it means doing that in ways that show no regard for the feelings or rights of other people. The aggressive person is out to get her way, no matter what it costs anyone else. People are surprised when I explain that aggression, like submission, is also often motivated by fear. Aggressive people can look confident as they come barging through life like a tank, but in fact they are often motivated by a fear of losing control of the situation. Despite appearances, they may be so lacking in self-confidence that they believe the only way to stand up for themselves successfully is to come on like a ton of bricks. The other common motivation for being aggressive is the fact that it seems to work, at least some of the time: you can scare some of the people some of the time. Of course, at other times being aggressive will earn you an aggressive response in return, like the conflict between aggressive programmes in Axelrod's research. Even when it seems to have got you your way, aggression costs. Many people feel embarrassed and guilty after an aggressive outburst, and it costs you in terms of your relationships. No one likes or respects a bully.

Some people will display both non-assertive styles at different times, because of their common base in a lack of real confidence. These people will most often be submissive, bottling up more and more bad feelings having locked themselves into losing behaviour patterns, until they finally reach Mount Vesuvius point and explode aggressively. Unfortunately, this explosion is often directed at the wrong person, someone whom you feel less threatened by and who is not really responsible for your accumulated aggravation. Even if you are exploding at someone more appropriate, an aggressive expression of your feelings will have both of the negative costs just mentioned, to your self-esteem and your relationships. So, although the two non-assertive styles have some short-term pay-offs, in temporarily postponing bad feelings or sometimes getting you what you want, in the long term they cost you much more than they gain and are not really successful.

Assertion means expressing your thoughts, opinions and feelings clearly, openly and non-defensively, making requests and refusing unacceptable requests, but doing that in ways that deliberately take account of the rights and feelings of other people. The underlying motivation is to show respect for both yourself and others. More than anything else, assertion is an expression of self-confidence: I know what I think or am prepared to accept, and I am confident of my ability to stand up for that, so I can afford to listen properly to you. It also involves realistic expectations about other people's likely reactions to your assertion, and of your ability to cope with those reactions.

The big pay-off for being assertive is to your self-esteem and your relationships, and I want to emphasise that these are the main goals of being assertive. At the end of an assertive interaction with someone, you are able to say to yourself: 'I'm pleased with how I handled that. I stood up for myself effectively, but I respected them, too.' Most other people will recognize that your assertion shows real respect for them, and will respond with respect for you, making your relationships more successful. In the process, you will have maximized your influence on the other people, but I emphasize that this is a secondary goal. Being assertive gives you your best chance of getting your way, most of the time, but it does not guarantee it. You will meet some people who are rigid, inflexible, dishonest, unscrupulous or just plain stubborn, and you won't always get a fair deal from the world. There are no real behaviour control techniques, so don't set out to control other people's behaviour; you are only setting yourself up for disappointment. Being assertive will give you consistently more influence over others, and that's all you need.

Preparing yourself to be assertive

Since assertion is an interpersonal style, the way you deal with people all of the time, it reflects your habitual way of thinking about others and your relationships with them. So, an important part of preparing yourself to be more assertive is to develop an assertive frame of mind. Responsible assertion rests on the two beliefs below. Read them over, and think about how they apply to you. The first is a straightforward observation, but it is important, because it is ultimately your motivation for putting in the effort to be assertive. The second looks obvious and some people are surprised it rates a mention but in practice you will find many people who act as if certain groups, like children, adolescents, women or employees, should not be asserting themselves. If you are going to be responsibly assertive, that means you expect others to be assertive back to you.

Assertive belief No. 1   Assertion, rather than submission, manipulation, or aggression, leads to more satisfying and successful interpersonal relationships and so enriches your life.

Assertive belief No. 2   Everyone is entitled to act assertively, and to express his or her honest thoughts, feelings and beliefs.

Incidentally, I might as well deal now with the old chestnut that usually gets raised during most assertion training by the group clown, being: 'But what happens when two people are assertive with each other? Don't you get stuck? (Chuckle, chuckle)' No, you don't. The question betrays a lack of understanding of the fundamental basis of responsible assertion, mutual respect. Two genuinely assertive people in a confrontation are much more likely to be able to listen to each other and negotiate a mutually acceptable agreement. Two aggressive people are more likely to get stubbornly stuck; two submissive people are more likely to compromise on a mutually unacceptable agreement; while an aggressive versus submissive confrontation will likely result in a one-way, unfair outcome. Later, I will give you suggestions on how to remain assertive with someone who is being aggressive or submissive.

To strengthen your assertive frame of mind, practise the self-statement below. I suggest you write it on a small card to carry around, and give yourself a refresher of assertive thinking several times a day, especially just before entering a situation in which you expect a confrontation. It's too long to use during a confrontation, but it's good preparation.

TO DEVELOP ASSERTIVE THINKING, PRACTISE SAYING TO YOURSELF: 'I expect to feel anxious when I assert myself, because most people do. I would feel disappointed if it doesn't work, and I might feel embarrassed or frightened if the other person overreacts; but I know I can cope with any of those feelings, and the chance of them happening is not a good reason for me to surrender my rights. It's important to me to assert myself reasonably and responsibly, so I will consider the rights and feelings of all the people in any situation before I assert myself. But if it is genuinely important to me, I will then assert myself.'

A second, good way of preparing yourself to be assertive is to observe other people's interpersonal styles. Discriminating which ones you think are assertive, submissive or aggressive will help you increase your awareness of the possible differences in your own interpersonal style. When you think you are watching a good example of assertion, see what you can learn from it. If he can do it, so can you.

The third and final preparation is to pinpoint situations in which you would like to be more assertive. These could be situations that already occur frequently in your life, that you think you presently approach submissively or aggressively, or they could be situations you have avoided until now because you didn't think you could handle them. Write out a short list of possible situations and then rank them in order of expected difficulty for you. You will start with the easiest and work up to the most difficult, because people learn best by succeeding. For each situation, imagine yourself working through the six steps I will describe next, but make sure you imagine yourself being successful. Imagine the bad ways others might react to your assertion, and imagine yourself handling these assertively, too. Imagined practice does transfer well to the real world, and you can take your time to get it right. Then try it out.

The six steps in being assertive

Step 1   Listen to others.

Responsible assertion involves showing respect for the rights and feelings of others in the situation. If you don't give them the chance to say their piece, or if you don't listen carefully, you can't know what they are on about and you can't begin to show real respect. If you think it would be helpful, go back and revise the suggestions on active listening in the previous chapter. In particular, 'listen' to the non-verbal parts of the other person's message; if she is indirectly expressing strong feelings, you should use communication skills to respond to those first.

If you have a strong urge to interrupt or talk over someone else because you disagree strongly with what he is saying (or more likely what you think he is going to say), kick yourself in the shins and think: 'I can listen to someone else's point of view without surrendering my own. I can always say what I want later.'

Step 2   Think about the situation.

Responsible assertion involves flexibility, choosing for assertion the situations where your personal rights are genuinely threatened, as distinct from situations that are just not quite how you would like them. It means not being unnecessarily or inappropriately assertive, and not being over-conscious of your rights. So, try to answer these three questions:

What are the rights of *all* of the people in this situation? Theirs? And mine?

Are my rights *really* threatened here?

Is this a situation where it's *genuinely* important to me to assert myself?

Only you can answer the last question, because your decision will reflect your personal values, interests and beliefs. An issue important to you may be unimportant to someone else, and vice versa. If you decide a situation is just unpleasant or inconvenient but not worth asserting yourself over, forget it. If you have trouble doing that, you may need to find out about mental relaxation. If you decide this is a situation where you want to be assertive, go on to the next step.

Both this and the next step involve a fair amount of thinking, and that's important if you want to assert yourself responsibly and effectively. But, in a confrontation, you may feel under pressure to say something quickly. Don't. A hasty response is more likely to be one you will regret later, as having been submissive, aggressive or off the real issue. You have a perfect right to think things over for a reasonable time, so use it. Firstly, say to yourself: 'I don't have to rush in. Give myself time to think about the situation properly.' Secondly, tell the others what you are doing: 'Wait a minute, please, I'd like to think about this for a minute or two.' If someone else has trouble coping with that, that's her problem.

Step 3 Work out how you see the situation.

At this stage, you will plan your initial assertive response. Later in this chapter, I will describe how to assert yourself under different circumstances. In particular, take time to decide what is really the important issue here *for you*, and assert yourself on that, not on some other, more obvious or less threatening issue. If you have the time, imagine how others are likely to respond to your initial assertive response, and work out your next assertive reply.

At this step, you will set your goals for asserting yourself in this situation, as realistically as possible. As I have already emphasized, the main goal of being assertive is just that, to see yourself being responsibly assertive. A possible second goal is to influence others to change some part of their behaviour, but only set that goal when you think there is a reasonable chance of obtaining it. Aiming to change the behaviour of people who obviously are not going to change only sets you up for disappointment.

Step 4 Assert yourself.

When it's an appropriate time for you to speak, make your initial assertive response. Try to stick to your assertive plan, but do listen to others to see if their responses suggest a change in your approach. Request more time to think, if you want it. If that puts you under pressure to respond quickly again, think to yourself: 'Relax; I have a perfect right to think about this.' If someone else has trouble coping with that, that's his problem.

Step 5   Think assertively.

As the discussion proceeds, you can help yourself stick to being assertive by giving yourself brief instructions:

If the other person becomes upset or angry, say to yourself: 'Stay calm, *I* don't have to get upset. If she wants to, that's her problem.'

If you become upset or angry, say to yourself: 'Relax; I'm in control.' Back this up with a calming response (from Chapter 4).

If you or someone else starts to wander off the topic or to introduce some other issue, say to yourself: 'Stick to the issue; don't get side-tracked,' and then you can say: 'I can see that (the new issue) is important to you, so let's discuss it next, but first I would like to finish this (the present issue).'

Step 6   Review the situation afterwards.

Later, when you have time to yourself, review how the situation went, to see what you can learn from it. If you were successful, which means *only* if you were able to stick to being responsibly assertive, *not* whether or not you got anyone else to change his behaviour, give yourself a pat on the back and file it all away in your memory as a successful formula.

Similarly, being unsuccessful means you were not able to stick to being assertive, but at some point became submissive or aggressive. Try to identify that point and what you did wrong; imagine how you could have handled it assertively instead. Then file that away for future use, and don't waste time and energy mulling over a single failure.

Assertion for different situations

In Step 3, you plan your initial assertive response, and the form of that will vary from situation to situation. I will now outline the basic form of an assertive approach to some commonly occurring situations.

Situation: Speaking up

This is the most basic form of assertion: saying clearly, promptly, calmly and firmly, how you feel or what you think. The key is to use I-language statements, like: 'I feel angry about not being consulted about a decision that affects me directly' or 'I would like our next holiday to be at the beach.' Even though basic assertion is simple, it is also important as the form of assertion most used for self-expression.

Situation: Making requests

I have been surprised at how reluctant some people are to make requests. 'Oh, I couldn't ask her to do that; she might not want to.' Notice the assumption underlying this reluctance is that, if you ask someone to do something, he must do it. Nonsense. You have a perfect right to make requests because other people have a perfect right to refuse your requests. The refuser must also be willing to wear the consequences of refusing, but she has the right to refuse. If you want someone to do something, the simplest and often most effective way of getting him to do it is to make a request.

Make your requests *clear and precise*, so that the other person knows exactly what you are asking. Vague requests set you up for dispute over whether they were met. Make your requests for *observable behaviours*, so there can be no doubt as to whether it has happened. Try to be *positive and non-defensive* in your manner, for example, by simply being courteous. You do have the right to make requests and I trust yours is a reasonable one. You should also have a *positive content*, that is, ask the other person to do something you want, not to stop doing something you don't want. Asking someone to stop doing something focusses on negative feelings and does not tell her what you want instead. Go straight to what you want instead and ask for that. While you are making your request, try to have reasonable *eye contact*, and *speak clearly and audibly*.

For example, you might request: 'Would you please bring the car around the front now.' Not, 'I don't suppose you would like to help' (defensive and vague), or 'When are you going to quit being lazy!' (aggressive, character-assassination, vague).

Situation: Refusing requests

As we have just discussed, you have a perfect right to refuse requests that are unacceptable to you, so long as you are also prepared to accept any consequences that may flow from your refusal. Make your refusals *clear*, so that the other person is in no doubt about your intentions. Again, be *non-defensive*: you do have the right to refuse requests. If you want to, offer an explanation for your refusal, but you are not necessarily obliged to do so. Most importantly, refuse *promptly*. If you are silent after receiving a request, it is easy for the other person to misinterpret your silence as acceptance of his request. If you later announce your refusal, his reaction may be all the stronger because he thought you had accepted. If you are not sure about whether or not to refuse a request, say that promptly, for example: 'Wait a minute, please, I would like to think about your request before I answer.' If you want to take longer than a minute or two to consider your reply, give the other person an indication of when you will have an answer, for example: 'I'll let you know after I have checked my diary (or before lunch, or whenever).' Again, try to have reasonable *eye contact, and clear, audible speech*.

For example, you might refuse the previous request: 'No, I'm sorry but I can't help you with the car right now. I have something else to do.' Not, 'Why should I?' (defensive), nor 'Well, I might get around to it later' (when you really don't intend to).

Situation: Negotiating

If someone makes a request that is unacceptable to you, or if you refuse an unacceptable request from someone else, you may *negotiate around the original request*, by each making counter-requests or counter-offers until you arrive at a mutually acceptable agreement. Professor Max Bazerman, of the Department of Organizational Behavior at Northwestern University, has suggested that five common mistakes in judgement block successful negotiations.

First, there is the mistake of approaching all negotiations as zero-sum situations, and not recognizing when win-win solutions are possible. I have discussed this mistake at length, and the problem-solving process below is a good way of avoiding it.

Second, there is the mistake of making what you think is a low offer, but it is in a field you are not familiar with. When the other side accepts immediately, you are left thinking, probably correctly, that your offer was really unnecessarily high. Professor Bazerman suggests you avoid this mistake by developing or buying expertise in the field in question, before negotiating.

Third, there is the mistake of continuing with a proposal that obviously has little chance of succeeding. Negotiators usually make this mistake because they tend to see things as supporting their point of view, and they are reluctant to be seen as backing down, even though the escalating conflict eventually costs them more. You can avoid this mistake by repeatedly doing a cost-benefit analysis of your present position. It also helps to avoid pushing your opponents into a corner or making them unnecessarily angry.

Fourth, there is the common mistake of being over-confident of the reasonableness of your position, and so of assuming others will see it as reasonable, too. This particularly applies to the use of independent arbitrators to resolve disputes, when most negotiators overestimate the chances of the arbitrator agreeing with them. You can avoid this mistake by getting an outside, expert opinion to counter your personal bias.

Fifth, there is the mistake of focusing on what you see as your possible losses in the negotiation, which will encourage you to hold out, again possibly losing more. Focusing on the possible gains in the negotiation — there are often both possible losses and gains — can help you to accept a realistic gain. Balance your judgement by considering both aspects of the negotiation, and present your proposals to the other side in terms of what they will gain. If your negotiations don't seem to be getting anywhere successfully, the problem-solving procedure below could be an effective way out.

Situation: Disagreeing with someone else's point of view

The key here is specifically to recognize the other person's point of view, but without surrendering your own. The basic form is: 'I see that's what you think; it's not how I see things.' By first acknowledging the other person's point of view you show respect for her; by sticking to your guns, you also show respect for yourself. For example: 'I can see that you would like to have our next holiday at the beach, but I think going to the mountains would suit all of the family better.'

Situation: Dealing with a persistent person

Responsible assertion involves not squashing others unnecessarily so, as a rule of thumb, *begin with what seems to be the minimum amount of assertion necessary, escalating to a firmer level only if your previous response was not sufficient.* With someone who is being unreasonably persistent, such as a very pushy salesperson, you can just keep repeating your assertive message over and over again. This technique, sometimes called the *broken record,* can be very effective in getting rid of pests, but because of the risk of it becoming aggressive you should use it only as a last resort.

For example, he says: 'Would you take care of my customers tomorrow, Carla?' You reply: 'No, Jake, I don't want to.' He says: 'But there's a really great game on that I want to see, and I know you aren't interested in football, so why not?' You reply: 'No, Jake, I can see you're keen to go to your football match, but I don't want to work on Saturday. I have my own plans.' He says: 'Don't be a rat. Whatever you've got on can wait, but this game only happens once a year.' You reply: 'Jake, when you won't take a polite "No" for an answer and keep pestering me like this, you're trying to interfere in my private life and that annoys me. I'd like you to ask someone else to look after your customers.'

Situation: Someone says one thing, but does something else

The key here is *objectively* to describe the other person's words and actions, *pointing out the contradiction* between them. It takes the general form: 'You said you would do this, but in fact you have done that.' If it is appropriate, you can add a request for change: 'I would like you to do this now, please.' Do *not* fall into the trap of interpreting the other person's motives or indulging in character-assassination; stick to an objective description of the other person's observable words and actions.

   For example, you might assert yourself: 'You said you would finish those contracts before you went home, but in fact you just left them. I would like you to do them now, please.'

Situation: Someone's actions are strongly influencing your feelings

You will recognize this as the situation calling for a levelling statement of the kind described in detail in Chapter 4: 'When you do X, the effect on me is Y, and I feel Z.' Again, if it is appropriate, you can add a request for change: 'I would prefer that you did Q instead, please.'
As I said in that chapter, if there are strong feelings involved in a situation, deal with the feelings first, or they will sabotage any other communication you attempt.

Situation: Presenting your ideas to a group

This applies to talking to boards, committees, meetings or any group, so that your ideas will be as influential as possible. The keys are to use appropriate *timing and tact*. If there is an agenda for the meeting, choose the items that are genuinely important to you, and save most of your talking for those items. If you have a lot to say about everything, you become part of the verbal wallpaper. When one of those items does come up, you will be more influential if you wait until a third to a half of the group have had their say, before you speak. You are showing your willingness to listen to others, and your confidence by not having to rush in. When you do speak, try to reflect something genuinely good about others' contributions before making your own, and again you are demonstrating your respect for other people's points of view.

For example, after waiting appropriately, you might say to the group: 'I thought Sam's idea of electric blue packaging was good as far as attractive presentation goes, and Mick is right that if we could make them ourselves it would save us some costs. However, I would like to suggest that getting some professionally made display cases would boost sales more than it would cost.'

Situation: Asserting yourself with someone being submissive

The risks here are that you may feel sorry for the submissive person, and back off into being submissive yourself, or you may find his submissiveness so frustrating that you become aggressive. In any case, his submissiveness may lead to you agreeing on something he does not genuinely accept and so may later not adhere to. The key here is to *level* about how you feel about his behaviour, adding a request for change if appropriate, but stick to your assertion.

The two kinds of submissiveness most difficult to handle are crying and withdrawal. Although crying is sometimes manipulative, it's usually best to take it as genuine, and reflect and validate the other person's distress (see Chapter 4). But then stick to your assertion. For example, you might say: 'I can see you're upset about this and I would feel bad about it if I were in your shoes. Still, we did agree that it was going to be done that way and I think you should stick to that agreement.' If the other person seems too distressed to continue with the discussion, take time out from it, but make sure that includes a specific appointment to return to the discussion. Withdrawal usually takes the form of silence accompanied by lots of body talk expressing bad feelings. Again, reflect and validate the other person's apparent feelings, while giving her room to speak if she wants to. For example, you might say: 'It looks to me as if you feel angry about this, and I can see why the situation would make you feel like that. But we do have to work out a solution that suits us both, so I'd appreciate knowing what you think.' For both crying and withdrawal, the advantage to your levelling is that you are giving the other person a good example of how to express his feelings more constructively.

Situation: Asserting yourself with someone being aggressive

This is the situation most feared by people who have previously been submissive but are now trying to be more assertive. 'But what will I do if she gets angry?' Well, let's get one thing clear: if the person you are asserting to does get angry, you won't die. You probably will feel embarrassed or awkward or even frightened, but there are no terminal cases of bad feelings. If necessary, go back and refresh the preparatory self-statement earlier in this chapter to help you adopt realistic expectations of the outcome of someone being angry at you.

The fact is, unless you are fortunate enough to be asserting yourself with someone who has also learned about assertion and communication and therefore knows how to respond in kind, when you do assert yourself you are most likely to get a defensive response of some sort, whether sullen submission or hostile aggression. No matter how reasonable your assertion may be nor how well you may do it, to an untrained person it will probably first appear to be an attack and he will probably be defensive. That's not a good reason for you not to be assertive, but it is a good reason for you to expect a defensive response at first and be prepared to handle it assertively.

If the other person looks or sounds angry, but isn't saying so, *reflect and validate her apparent feelings*, so inviting her to level about them so they can be dealt with openly first. Then stick with your original assertion. For example, 'You seem to be angry about this, and I can see why you might feel like that. But I still think you should pass on my messages, like we agreed.'

If the other person responds with personal abuse or by raising other issues to attack you, *don't side-tracked* into a slanging match or on to red herrings. Still reflect and validate his apparent feelings, but stick to your assertion. For example, he says: 'Well, it's typical of your rigidity that you want your messages straight away, like you always want your letters in duplicate.' You reply: 'I can understand you feel angry about this, but the issue I'd like to settle now is reliably getting my messages. If there's a problem about duplicating my letters, let's discuss that next.'

If the other person is aggressively trying to get you to back down on some point, use the technique above of *specifically recognizing her point of view while sticking to yours*. If the other person's argument rests on unstated assumptions that you think are questionable, *point out his underlying assumptions and your disagreement*. For example, you might say: 'I can see that your suggestion of making the display cases ourselves represents a cost saving, but you are assuming we can do a professional-looking job, and I don't think that's true.'

Some people respond aggressively to your assertion by asking questions or trying to debate the issue with you. As a rule of thumb, *don't answer questions while asserting*, except in the rare case that some further information is genuinely called for. A question is more likely to be an attack on you and should be reflected as such. For example, he says: 'Well, did you always stick to the plans when you were working in assembly?' You reply: 'It sounds to me as if you think I am asking higher standards of work from you than I would from myself.'

Don't be drawn into a debate, an intellectual, verbal competition in which someone must lose. Reflect the other person's feelings and stick to your original assertion. For example, she says: 'It does seem to me that there is an important principle here, about deciding the priority of different office tasks and who decides those priorities. How do you think the office should be run?' You reply: 'I can understand you feel angry about this, but I'm not going to argue principles with you. If they are important to you, let's discuss them at the next staff meeting. Right now, I'm concerned that you have not passed on my messages as we agreed.'

Solving problems

At first glance, decision-making and problem-solving may appear to be two ways of saying the same thing, but they are not. There are many ways of making decisions, ranging from the instant, snap decision made inside one person's head to a majority consensus resolution of a major conflict after long discussions amongst the parties involved. My intention is to encourage co-operative decision-making: when a decision is made by any method, there has been participation in the process by all of those involved in the decision.

Some problems and conflicts disappear with just good communication, being able to say: 'I see that's how you think about this; it's not how I think about it, but I accept it's how you do.' This is mostly true of conflicts of *values* and *feelings*, when it is unlikely and usually unnecessary that anyone will change his opinions or feelings about the issue.

Conflicts over *goals* and *wants* cannot usually be handled so easily because, after you have listened to and validated each other's values or feelings, there is still a substantive issue to be resolved: what will be done or how will it be done. Some of these problems can be resolved using assertion skills, particularly making and negotiating around requests. All of these are examples of co-operative decision-making, because the final decision results from mutually respectful discussion amongst the affected parties. But some problems are too big, too complicated, too new or involve too much conflict to be dealt with using only communication or assertion skills. Then a more powerful problem-solving process is called for, and that is the subject of this discussion.

How not to solve problems

Whether they recognize it or not, people are solving problems from time to time, even if it's only who will put the kettle on next. Because it is such a routine part of anyone's life you may well not notice when some problem-solving is occurring, and that could mean you use one of the traditional but less effective approaches to problem-solving. I want to describe these now to help you recognize when opportunities are occurring for using the process set out below. The more aware you are of your chances to do good problem-solving, and the more deliberately you follow the procedure below, the better your solutions and the higher your success rate will be.

It's what we've always done. There is such a thing as wisdom, good ideas built up through experience, and it is sometimes expressed in traditions. There is also such a thing as rigidity, based on laziness or a fear of the new, and it is sometimes expressed in traditions. Given the rate of technological change today, the traditional way of doing things may well not be the best, for either work efficiency or job satisfaction. The best way of not throwing the baby out with the bathwater is to examine traditional practices with an open mind, and the problem-solving process below is a good way of doing that.

Because I said so! The 'boss' may be someone who occupies a formal position of authority, such as a manager, foreman or supervisor. Or the 'boss' may be someone who has assumed a dominant role in a group, such as a committee or even your family, perhaps by being aggressive while others in the group are submissive. When a problem arises, the boss decides what will be done, perhaps after some consultation, but even then it's clear whose decision it is. You will recognize this as the most common approach to problem-solving in most workplaces. Many bosses are initially threatened by the idea of co-operative decision-making because they think it will lead to their losing power. That power is illusory and attempts to wield it, by threats and coercion, get mixed results at best while inviting retaliation, open or hidden. Decisions imposed on people without their genuine participation do not receive whole-hearted support or commitment and so are unlikely to be carried through successfully.

It's getting late. Without the application of good inter-personal skills, problem-solving can easily bog down into endless repetition of the same ideas, especially in situations of conflict, with each participant trying to defend her own preferred solution. The process may be further protracted by people raising other issues, red herrings, or rambling personal anecdotes. Eventually, most people are bored and fed up with the lack of progress, and any decision is seized upon to end the discussion. This is making deci-sions 'by attrition', since it amounts to solving a problem by wearing down people's resistance to other ideas. It also generally wears down their interest and involvement; bored and fed-up people are unlikely to make good solutions or to feel good about whichever solution was finally made.

If your problem-solving is occurring at formal meetings, I suggest limiting your meetings to an hour or two. If you aren't getting through your agenda in that time, first check your meeting process (see *Working Together*) to see if your use of the appropriate skills could improve. If you think your meetings are running as well as reasonably possible, but you still can't complete your agendas, then you may need to schedule meetings more often.

Let's compromise. People in conflict are often advised to compromise, and a willingness to do so is often seen as a sign of reasonableness. Compromise properly means to settle a dispute by all parties conceding some part of their original goals, and it can *sometimes* be an appropriate way of breaking deadlocks. Because everyone gives up something, it can seem fair and demonstrate willingness to try to accommodate each other's goals. But notice that it involves everyone giving up some part of their goals; it is therefore a lose-lose solution, in contrast to the win-lose outcomes described above for problem-solving by domination. By compromis-ing, everyone has lost something and the size of that loss may be finally seen by some as too great. Then you have at best reluctant acceptance of the solution, at worst a change of mind and no solution after all.

Compromise also runs the risk of reducing creativity and producing solutions that are bland enough not to offend anyone, but are also mediocre or silly. The advantages to the problem-solving process below are that it should generate win-win solutions, where everyone involved thinks they have gained by the solution adopted, and it should maximize creativity to produce effective solutions.

Preparing for problem-solving

I suggest that it is essential, if co-operative problem-solving is going to work properly, that *all of those taking part have had the chance to learn the skills of communication, anger-management, conflict resolution, assertion and problem-solving beforehand*. I have seen a number of organizations that claim to use the procedure called 'management by objectives'. One of the key ideas in this procedure is that a manager will collaborate with each of his subordinates in setting the objectives that the worker will achieve over the next year, at the end of which his performance is evaluated against those objectives. The principle is fine, but in practice, because most of the people participating have not learned the necessary interpersonal skills, what you get is another ill-disguised version of the boss telling the worker what to do. If you want people genuinely to participate in a discussion, you must first make sure they know how and feel confident about doing it.

If you are doing your problem-solving in a meeting, some preparation will help that, too. *Circulate an agenda and any supporting information beforehand*, so that everyone taking part has had time to become familiar with the problems to be tackled. *Arrange for necessary information to be available* at the meeting, whether that means having certain documents or some expert adviser present. If you find, while tackling a problem, that you lack important information, it's best to postpone solving that problem until the information is obtained, if that is possible. *Plan how much time to spend on each agenda item*, reflecting the urgency and importance of the item, so that all business will be covered within the allocated time, but be willing to be flexible if necessary. *Rank items in order of urgency and importance* and show them in that order on the agenda, but again be willing to be flexible to accommodate strong feelings.

Finally, *decide who should be involved*. A committee or board or similarly formal body will not necessarily be the most appropriate group to discuss every problem. As a rule of thumb, the people who should take part in solving a particular problem should be those with important relevant information or skills, or who are part of the problem, or who will carry out or have major influence over the solution. Others less directly involved but who may still be affected by the solution can be consulted during the process and informed of the outcome. The risk in making all of the members of a committee discuss all problems is that some people will be bored by and have little to offer towards some issues, which will not enhance your problem-solving. Be willing to set up working parties, selected along the lines above, to tackle such problems and recommend solutions.

Co-operative problem-solving

The problem-solving process consists of six steps and, for maximum effectiveness, you should keep the steps clearly separate. One of the reasons that conflicts can become heated and drawn out is that people are frightened a decision they don't want is going to be inflicted on them against their wishes, or a decision will be made before they have had a say in it. If everyone knows the six-step process, and any chairperson makes it clear that the steps are being dealt with sequentially and fully, then everyone knows that a solution will not be chosen until Step 4, and that there will have been a full opportunity for everyone to have a say in the preceding three steps. This takes a lot of the steam out of the situation and allows people to devote their energies to the actual problem-solving, rather than to defending themselves against a perceived attack on their rights.

If you have a chairperson, she has a big contribution to make to the success of your group's problem-solving. Assertively but tactfully, she needs to keep the discussion on the current topic, focussed on the present step only, and she needs to prevent members getting ahead or trailing behind. Ideally, she will also facilitate good use of the interpersonal skills, by setting the example, and by reflecting feelings back to group members, with the suggestion that they also use appropriate skills. Effective problem-solving needs people to speak up and to listen, and may well arouse strong feelings, so all of the skills discussed so far will be needed.

Step 1   Define the problem.

This is a vital step, since it sets the task to come, yet it is often done hastily with the result that the problem is not solved satisfactorily. Defining the problem accurately can take up to half of the total problem-solving time, especially in conflict situations, but that will be time well spent.

It is *essential* that the problem is defined in terms of wants, and not in terms of possible solutions, to maximize creativity and prevent unnecessary conflict. Defining a problem in terms of possible solutions blinds you to other possible solutions which may have been better. And it creates conflict when people define the problem in terms of mutually exclusive solutions. For example, 'The problem here is which one of us gets to use the car on Saturday night. I need it to get to my friends' place.' 'Well, so do I. I need the car to visit my parents.' This kind of conflict goes nowhere, because each of the participants has defined the problem in terms of her preferred solution, using the family car, which is in conflict with the other person's preferred solution. They will just waste time and energy trying to defend their original preferred solutions.

To get at the wants behind solutions and break this deadlock, *ask what the person wants his proposed solution for*. In our example, one person might say: 'I need the car for transport to my friends' place.' The other person might say: 'I need the car for transport to my parents' place.' Their actual wants are transport, and only one solution to that want is having the family car; there are plenty of other ways of getting transport that will not be in conflict. If you are not sure that you have discovered a person's real wants in a problem situation, keep asking why she wants her proposed solution. If you can find an answer to that 'why', the answer is more likely to be real want in this situation.

Once you have defined what each person wants from the situation, *combine the separate statements into a single definition of the problem*. From our example above, the two people would define their problem as wanting transport for each of them to their respective destinations. This combined statement of everybody's wants is the starting point for the next step, and it guarantees you are looking for win-win solutions. If the definition of the problem is getting too bulky to fit into a single reasonable statement, you should probably be breaking the problem down into two or more sub-problems, to be tackled one at a time.

Step 2 Brainstorm possible solutions.

This is the step that gets your creativity going, and gives you the best chance of coming up with a really good solution. If you look around your workplace or your home, chances are that more than half the gadgets you see were created by brainstorming, because it is now a well-established technique for solving design problems. Brainstorming means quickly creating as many solutions as possible for the defined problem. The sole aim is to *produce as many solutions as you can imagine*, without any reservations at this stage.

To get maximum creativity, follow these guidelines. *Keep the brainstorming session brief.* Usually about five or ten minutes is sufficient. Have *no evaluation or criticism* of solutions, so as not to discourage any contributions. *Don't explain* or ask anyone else to explain suggestions, as this only blocks the creative flow. *Include (some) silly ideas*, partly because they can act as springboards for good ideas, and partly to relieve tension which can further stimulate creativity. *Use others' ideas as springboards*, adding to or expanding on them. These synergistic interactions are a major factor in group creativity. *List every suggestion*, in a few of the proposer's own words, but don't tie suggestions to people by listing names. This is a co-operative exercise. Again, your chairperson has an important task keeping people to these guidelines, but it's worth it in terms of creating good solutions.

Step 3   Evaluate the possible solutions.

The chairperson reads out each of the suggested solutions, one at a time, and the group proposes possible advantages and disadvantages for each solution. These pros and cons are briefly listed next to each solution. Again, this is a co-operative exercise, with everyone free to suggest pros or cons for every solution, not just out to defend his own suggestions. If further explanation is wanted of any suggestion, now is the time for it, when its turn for discussion comes up.

Do accept expressions of disagreement. Sometimes people are so scared of conflict that they try to brush it under the table as soon as any looms. This will inhibit people from saying what they really think, can leave strong feelings unexpressed and therefore not dealt with, and may lead to mediocre decision-making by compromise. Assertive expression of disagreement will hurt no one.

When the flow of pros and cons for a particular suggestion has run out, each member of the group should give a rating to that solution, of '+' or '−'. These ratings should be applied properly, if you are later going to achieve a realistic consensus. A plus rating should mean: 'Yes, I would be willing to try this solution.' It does *not* necessarily mean I think this is the best solution or even that I think it will work, only that I am willing to give it a try. A minus rating should mean: 'No, I have strong objections to this solution and I would not be willing to give it a try.' It should *not* mean only that I don't like this solution or that I think there are better ones. A minus rating amounts to your personal veto, so it should be used sparingly, only when you have genuinely strong objections to a suggestion.

Step 4   Choose a solution.

Realistic consensus means choosing a solution that everyone is willing to try, *not* one that everyone unanimously agrees is the best. Unanimity of opinion can take forever to achieve, and is unnecessary for successful problem-solving. You are looking for unanimity of willingness to try the chosen solution. It is not unusual finally to combine several suggested solutions, so as to meet all of the wants expressed in the definition of the problem. You may need to accept a solution with less than unanimous support, but I would be wary of proceeding with a solution that someone has strong objections to. The risk is that she will later have insufficient commitment to carry the solution through, or may even sabotage it.

If you cannot select a solution with realistic consensus, you recycle the problem-solving process, going back to Step 1 — are you stalled because someone has some previously unidentified want? — and Step 2 — is there some other solution possible that everyone is willing to try? It is possible that you may come up against a problem for which you cannot reach a solution by realistic consensus, usually because it involves sharp conflict. Your group may decide to break such deadlocks by a simple majority vote, or by asking one person — the manager, the director, or whoever — to listen to both sides and then choose one, putting the onus on the supporters of that solution to make it work. Such deadlocks are rare but possible, so you should choose your method for breaking them *before* one happens.

Step 5   Plan to implement your solution.

This step is surprisingly often missed; many people have had some introduction to problem-solving but stop after selecting a solution, and then wonder why nothing happens. A solution is a plan of action for solving a problem, and it is essential that you now translate it into concrete action. You should now answer the following questions: *Who* will do *what? Where? By when?* What *resources* are needed? *Who* will obtain them? *How?* From *where?* It may be desirable for one person to take responsibility for following the whole solution through, coordinating different contributions and seeing that they all occur as planned. You have not completed this step until you have a detailed plan of action, which is understood by the people who will carry it out.

Step 6 Implement your plan.

Follow your plan through, one step at a time, and evaluate the outcome in terms of the goals you originally set back in Step 1. You should also look at the wider impact of your solution, on other aspects, such as productivity or job satisfaction. Sometimes a solution may be successful in terms of the problem, but have other, unforeseen consequences that may need further problem-solving. If you are not satisfied that the solution has met the goals set in Step 1, or if it is having unacceptable negative side-effects, recycle the problem-solving process. Look carefully at what is unsatisfactory about the outcome and feed that information back into the process, too. It may lead you to redefine the problem, or it may prompt some new solutions, or change some people's attitudes about which solutions to try. It can also be helpful to review the problem-solving *process*, and how it is affecting feelings and relationships within the group. If it is working properly, it should be developing feelings of co-operation, involvement and commitment, and thus motivation.

Co-operative problem-solving is also known as collaborative decision-making, or worker participation, or industrial democracy. Whatever name you give it, there is clear and concrete evidence that it is the path to success for organisations, including profitable enterprises.

6 | THE TRUTH ABOUT
MOTIVATION

To continue my aim of starting again from basics, to get rid of the claptrap and deadwood that have accumulated around the concepts of success and motivation, I thought I would start this chapter with another definition from the dictionary. What a disappointment! The dictionary regards motivation as a motivating; a providing of a motive. That's a good example of the circular thinking in this field that I intend to demolish in this chapter. They get closer to the popular mark with their definition of 'motivated': 'ambitious; determined; energetic'. Now I hear some bells ringing. That's what you bought this book for, because you're ambitious, because you want to be determined and energetic. Well, I have some sad news for you. You won't achieve any of that by reading about motivation. Why not? Simple; it doesn't exist.

Motivation is a fairy story

In psychological circles the field of motivation developed as an attempt to explain *why* behaviour occurs, a not unreasonable question. Some early psychologists picked up the existing notion of *instincts* and began to propose that humans, like other animals, had certain instincts. This approach reached its fullest flowering in the proposal of such instincts as 'hair-combing', to explain why people comb their hair. The idea of instincts has not worked too well, even in understanding the simpler behaviour of non-human animals, but it was usually taken to imply that an urge to behave this way was genetically inherited or biologically built in. If that were so, you would have to wonder why some humans do not comb their hair, a question that many parents would like answered.

Instincts gave way to *drives* and the closely related idea of *needs*. People need food to stay alive, so they have a hunger drive to make them go out and get food. This approach has some appeal and even a bit more utility than instinct theory in trying to understand the behaviour of rats and cockroaches. But even amongst non-humans, it pretty quickly gets into strife. What need is a well-fed, well-watered, sexually-satisfied rat meeting when it sniffs its way around a maze, apparently exploring? What drive urges your pet dog to keep retrieving the stick you keep throwing away? What need or drive explains the behaviour of an overweight person eating more than he needs, or an anorexic starving herself to death?

To cope with these troublesome observations, the motivation theorists had to propose higher order needs or drives, ones that did not serve the survival of the individual or even the species. So you wind up with psychologists like Abraham Maslow proposing a hierarchy of five levels of needs in humans, ranging from physiological and safety needs up to needs for self-esteem and 'self-actualization' (the realization of your potential). That well-known Viennese neurologist, Sigmund Freud, originally proposed one major drive in humans, the *libido*, usually misrepresented as a sex drive, but really a more general 'life' drive (like the rest of psychoanalysis, it was all a bit vague and woolly). After the First World War he felt obliged to propose a second major drive, *thanatos*, the death and destruction drive, to explain the massive killing that had occurred. And therein he exemplifies the essential weakness of most so-called motivational theory: he proposed thanatos *after* he had observed the death and destruction of the First World War to explain why it had occurred. He could not predict the behaviour *beforehand* from his theory.

Round and round the motivation bush

Traditional motivational concepts have in fact been circular *descriptions* of behaviour, not *explanations*. Watch: why does this man comb his hair? Because he has an instinct for hair-combing. How do we know he has an instinct for hair-combing? Because he combs his hair.

Too easy? Try this one: Why does this woman strive to build her self-esteem? Because she has a need for self-esteem. How do we know she has a need for self-esteem? Because she strives to build it. The concepts of motivation turn out to be no more than shorthand descriptions of the behaviour they were alleged to explain. Their uselessness to the serious science of psychology was their inability to predict future behaviour, because that is the essence of scientific theory. It can predict reasonably accurately before the event, not just appear to explain after the event.

Despite their fall from scientific favour, these motivational 'theories' have been popular because of their ability to supply an apparent explanation. Psychoanalysis is infallible, in that sense. No matter what a person does, you can concoct a psychoanalytic explanation for the behaviour, *after* you have observed it. As a predictor of future behaviour, it's a flop (and its success rate as a psychotherapy leaves a lot to be desired, especially in terms of cost-effectiveness). But as a supplier of glib explanations, it can never be wrong, a characteristic which I think explains its popularity with some therapists.

So traditional motivational theory and research are not going to be much help in getting you moving down the road to success. If that's so, what do they talk about at all those 'motivation' seminars. What indeed?

The pop psychology of motivation

If the traditional psychology of motivation has fallen into disuse, superseded by more refined ideas (to be considered shortly), what has pop psychology to offer? To be fair, I have not attended many 'motivation' seminars, only those to which I have been invited as a speaker. There may be some popular seminar speakers who do offer suggestions of practical and significant value, even if I haven't heard them. Decide for yourself, using the criteria I suggested in Chapter 1. But I must report the suggestions I heard boiled down to a few tricks intended to get people to try harder, probably worth trying but hardly deserving the accompanying fanfares.

Yet, as I described in Chapter 1, many of the participants think these seminars are great. So great, that they keep going back to more. Why? If, as I suggest, most 'motivation' seminars offer little of practical or significant value, why do so many participants think they were worth going to? Apart from the reasons I proposed earlier — the need to tell yourself you haven't wasted your money, and the real difficulty of critically evaluating something outside your own field of expertise — I think there is one other major reason for the popularity of 'motivation' seminars. They are exciting.

And deliberately so. The 'motivational' speakers I have seen are making very deliberate use of emotionally arousing techniques, in how they speak, how they move and stand, what they wear, and in their often elaborate audio-visual accompaniments. Not that they need to try too hard. So long as you have a bit of hide, it is not difficult to whip up a bit of crowd reaction, as politicians and medicine men have known for centuries. Throw in a few jokes (to show you are a fun person), a few anecdotes (to show you are like your audience), and a few key words or phrases (to evoke an easy emotional response), and you are away. It is not hard to make a seminar presentation that people will walk out from, feeling aroused. If you use the right verbal prompts, like 'success' and 'motivation', they will come out believing they have just been 'motivated'. But see how long it lasts.

In using emotion to sell lightweight ideas about motivation, the pop 'psychologists' (very few of them are qualified psychologists) have accidentally tripped across a real link. Emotions do play a key role in human motivation, although not just as a means of selling seminars.

Motivation, emotion and thinking

The heyday of 'needs' theories of motivation was the heyday of behaviourism, the self-conscious attempt by psychology to prove it was a respectable science by only studying observable phenomena, the stimulus impinging on the organism and the response that followed. What went on inside the organism was the business of physiologists and other biologists, and psychologists should keep their noses out and clean. To strengthen our scientific standing, we should do as much as possible of our research inside the laboratory. Unfortunately, few humans were willing to live in laboratories or to go without food or water or sex to establish the appropriate needs and drives, so psychologists studied a lot of rats and similar animals with fewer civil rights or less ability to complain.

I don't want to give you the impression that I feel all this scientific endeavour was wasted. It did generate some useful psychological principles, particularly for training rats, but of less direct applicability to people. You see, we are not just giant rats (whatever you may think of some of your acquaintances). In particular, humans think and rats don't. And thinking turns out to be both a most human part of our psychology, and an important one.

The psychologist who has done an excellent job of humanizing the learning theory of behaviourism is Professor Arthur Staats, at the University of Hawaii. His theory, social behaviourism, combines the well-established psychological discoveries of classical behaviourism with the human behaviour of thinking and the human characteristic of being a social animal. It provides a far better account of human learning and motivation than anything before it. In essence, Staats says stimuli — objects, people, events — have motivational impact on us only because of our attitudes towards them. When we meet a stimulus, our attitude towards it, which reflects our previous experience with that and similar stimuli, determines how we feel about it, bringing our emotions into play. If the emotions are mostly good, we will strive to increase our contact with the stimulus; if the feelings are mostly bad, we will strive to reduce our contact with the stimulus. And there you have motivated behaviour, mediated by our emotions, determined by our attitudes. If you accept this approach to human motivation, then you can see that attitudes will play a key role in building and maintaining your motivation.

One attitude in particular plays a crucial role in motivation, and we will consider it now. I dismissed the pop psychology approach to motivation as often consisting of just tricks to get people to try harder. The tricks may or may not be genuinely helpful, but the question is a reasonable one. How do you get someone — yourself or someone else — to try harder? What *really* determines how hard you try? Easy: your self-efficacy.

Self-efficacy

My what? At this point my friends would accuse me of talking psychobabble, but I'm not. I share their dislike for unnecessary jargon, the retreat behind polysyllabic words to express something that could be said in plain language, usually to boost the speaker's status or identify him as a 'professional'. A new word is justified, I think, to express a new idea, a concept for which there is no already existing term. So now it's time for you to learn your new word for the day, with the bonus that it is also the secret of human motivation.

Your self-efficacy is your belief in your ability to carry out a specific task to achieve a specific goal.

There are several key points to this definition. First, note that your self-efficacy is a belief; it is an attitude towards yourself, an idea about your capacities that you hold to be true. So we are again emphasizing the essential role that thinking plays, not only in motivation but in human psychology in general, and the desirability of making your thinking as realistic as possible. Inflate your self-efficacy with unrealistically high ideas regarding your abilities and you are setting yourself up for a discouraging fall flat on your face. Deflate your self-efficacy with unrealistically low ideas about your abilities and you will talk yourself out of potential successes.

Second, note that self-efficacy is a much more refined concept than vague old notions like self-esteem or self-confidence. It is your confidence about a specific task and a specific outcome. This degree of specificity explains the puzzling anomaly you will have seen, of the apparently confident person who is suddenly and surprisingly reluctant to tackle a new task. If you have watched someone, trying hard and performing well in areas for which she has high self-efficacy, you may be surprised when she suddenly makes little or no attempt in a different area. 'I thought Jane had more confidence than that!'

The converse also occurs. If you have mostly seen someone putting a (predictably) weak effort into an area where he lacks self-efficacy, you can then be surprised by how enthusiastically he tackles a different area for which he has high self-efficacy.

You may have high self-efficacy in some areas of your life and low in others. 'I'm a great cook, but I'm boring company.' 'I'm a whiz at selling, but I can't stand up to the boss's unreasonable demands.' 'I'm a pretty good parent and a loyal spouse, but I'm hopeless in bed.' If that were you, chances are you would willingly try out a new recipe, but you would hide in the kitchen when the company came. You would front potential customers, even when you weren't getting sales, but dodge the boss back at the office. You would try to solve a problem with your kids, but get a headache or be very tired at bedtime. Notice how your self-efficacy would be influencing your behaviour.

Your self-efficacy determines what you will try, how hard you will try, and how long you will persist with those efforts.

Now you can see why your self-efficacy is so central to your motivation. High self-efficacy and you are in there giving it a try, a hard try, and a long try, motivating yourself. Low self-efficacy, and you may not try at all, or if you do, you won't try very hard nor for very long, with little apparent motivation. So, the secret to building your motivation in any area of your life is to build your self-efficacy for the relevant tasks and goals. How do you do that?

Your self-efficacy is mostly influenced by four factors:
- **accomplishments**
- **modelling**
- **verbal persuasion**
- **your level of arousal.**

So these four factors offer four means of increasing your self-efficacy.

Building self-efficacy with accomplishments

The first and probably most important way of building self-efficacy is to give yourself success experiences. That might sound obvious but there are, in fact, two essential components to success, at least as far as building self-efficacy is concerned. The first is reasonably obvious, but the second is neglected by some people. First, you must have some actual successes. Second, you must see them as successes.

No. 1 tip for motivation   Use trial-and-success learning.

Despite the popularity of the phrase, there is no such thing as trial-and-error learning, other than in a very restricted sense. All making an error tells you is that you got it wrong; it does not tell you what you should have done instead or what would have been right. In a situation where the number of choices open to you is very limited — do I turn left or right? — getting your first choice wrong does make it fairly likely you will get it right next time. But how many situations are you trying to handle successfully where you have only two choices? Most human situations offer you many choices, both simultaneously and sequentially. Knowing you got your last move wrong is not going to narrow down by much your choices for the next move.

The other problem with making mistakes is that it discourages you; make enough of them and you are likely to get fed up and stop trying. There goes *your* motivation. Just as accomplishments build self-efficacy, failures reduce it. Any attempt really to use a process of trial-and-error learning would likely be slow, haphazard and increasingly unmotivated.

Success, by contrast, encourages you, it makes you feel good, it builds your self-efficacy so you are more likely to try again. Since you now have a fair idea of what to do that will be right, you are more likely to be successful again. In the next chapter I will discuss goal-setting in some detail, as an important motivational device, but one point needs to be made here, the use of sub-goals.

If a goal is very large or distant, you should set sub-goals along the way towards it. Any well-designed programme for change — whether you call it therapy, education, training or personal improvement — uses this principle. There may be a clear final goal — to master a new skill, earn a particular qualification or award, or improve some facet of your life or relationships, or whatever — but you can see that realistically it's going to take a while to achieve. How do you keep yourself motivated along the way? One important method is to set sub-goals, intermediate goals that are far enough apart to keep you moving, to keep you progressing, but close enough to keep you enjoying the success of achieving the next one reasonably frequently. That also means the amount of change or improvement required to get from one sub-goal to the next is reasonable, so that you are highly likely to succeed at each one. Don't underestimate the importance of this principle of a graded approach to important goals, to keep you motivated and trying.

The other obvious requisite for getting it right is to know what to do. In Chapters 4 and 5 I have introduced you to some essential interpersonal skills — communication, conflict-resolution, assertion, negotiation, and problem-solving — because they are often the skills for success not taught in most training programmes. If you have not already done so, do make an honest estimate of which ones *you* need to strengthen and take the time to do so. Not all the tasks in your life will require you to deal with other people, but most will, and you will need those skills to be successful at those tasks. I also repeat my earlier point that you will naturally also need whatever skills are relevant to the task in hand. To give yourself a reasonable chance of being successful, get the information, training or advice necessary to master those task-relevant skills, too.

No. 2 tip for motivation   Use a realistic definition of success.

No matter how well you do, it only becomes an accomplishment for building self-efficacy when *you* tell yourself you did well. You must recognize your successes and take them to heart. Remember the definition of success I introduced earlier: to have done your personal best, at this stage, given your genes, your past experiences and your present situation. If you need to refresh those ideas, take another look at Chapter 3, but then apply them. Whenever you have done your personal best, given those realistic limitations, recognize your successes and give yourself a pat on the back. 'Hey, I did that as well as I could expect. Good for me! That's a success.'

You may well decide you can do better in the future — it was your realistic best *at this stage* — with more training or coaching or practice. But that does not lessen your present success which should be recognized by you in the present.

Setting yourself impossible goals and perfectionist standards must cause you to fail *in your eyes*, no matter what anyone else may say about how well you did. This will chip away at your self-efficacy until you either give up trying, or drive yourself into the Type A Behaviour Pattern, neither outcome being part of my definition of success.

Building self-efficacy through modelling

Forgive my introducing another psychological term but again there is no direct common equivalent. You will probably have guessed that by 'modelling' I am not referring to people of freakish appearance — fashion models are statistically improbable — being paraded as some desirable norm for the rest of us, as a means of selling us clothes, cosmetics, or whatever.

For a psychologist, modelling means learning a new behaviour by watching someone else do it successfully. The nearest common equivalent term would be imitation, but imitation usually occurs immediately and seems to be mostly a way for the imitator to try out the imitated behaviour, to see what it feels like, rather than a deliberate attempt to achieve the goal of the imitated behaviour. Some imitation also seems to be intended more for social purposes, such as in children's play or in one adult teasing another by mimicking him. Again the goal is not that of the original behaviour.

Modelling may be delayed, even by years. A compelling example of this is the way many of us start to deal with our children in much the same way as our parents dealt with us, years ago, even when we may have vowed at the time, 'I'll never do that to my kids when I grow up.' Modelling also depends on your observing the model being successful at the behaviour, being rewarded for it, so that your subsequent attempts at the behaviour are also aimed at achieving the same success, earning the same reward. This is purposeful, motivated behaviour, not just exploratory or sociable. It also depends on the degree to which you identify with the model: the more you see her as being like you, at least in terms of the factors you see as relevant, the more strongly you will model your behaviour on hers.

Modelling certainly occurs in some non-humans, as you can see in the quite deliberate teaching of hunting skills by adult predators to their young. But at least some psychologists believe it plays a particularly important role in human learning, and it is the second of the factors you can use to build self-efficacy. Watching someone else successfully doing the task you wish to master, identifying with that person and enjoying her reward vicariously, can increase your belief in your ability to be successful at that task, too.

No. 3 tip for motivation   Be a success copycat!

Make deliberate, planned use of this factor. Look for people who are good examples of the successes you wish to achieve. You are not looking for envy: we have already dealt with the foolishness of inappropriately comparing yourself with others. You are looking for ideas — 'How exactly did he do that?' — and for encouragement — 'If she can do it, so can I!'

Make judicious use of modelling. Remember it is most effective if you can identify closely with the model, so you are looking for someone similar to yourself in the characteristics relevant to the task in hand. Picking a model who is significantly different from you may lower your self-efficacy — 'Well, of course *he* can do it, he's much stronger than *I* am. I've got no hope.' Or it may set you up for a failure, when you try to model yourself on someone with very different abilities, past history or present circumstances, and the failure will in turn lower your self-efficacy.

No. 4 tip for motivation   Show me!

In using modelling to build your self-efficacy, don't be afraid to ask for demonstrations of success from potential models. Most people are flattered by such requests and happy to oblige. Sure, making a polite but assertive request for a demo may make you feel a little anxious or embarrassed, and you probably would feel bad if the other person turned you down or reacted badly. But, as we discussed in Chapter 5, you *can* cope with all of those feelings and the chance of their happening is not a good enough reason for you to miss out, in this case, on a potentially good learning opportunity.

No. 5 tip for motivation   Look at yourself!

The other source of good models consistently ignored by some people is you, yourself. Look at your past successes, as we are now defining them realistically. If you did it well once, you have a good chance of succeeding again. Even when you are facing a new task, have you previously been successful with something similar? 'Well, this looks tricky, but it *is* like the one I handled last month. If I could handle that one, I can probably do okay with this one, too.' Of course, you will more easily be a good model for yourself if you have been clearly identifying your realistic successes as they occurred.

Building self-efficacy by persuasion

A number of times I have referred to the crucial role played in human behaviour by our thoughts, our self-talk, and this is a further example. In the original research into self-efficacy, the psychologists involved focussed on how someone else could verbally persuade you into higher self-efficacy, could talk you into believing you had a chance of succeeding, a possibility used by generations of sports coaches, and one I will consider further in the next chapter. If you do enjoy the support of someone else's encouragement, by all means use it. If it is potentially available, by all means do make an assertive request for it.

No. 6 tip for motivation   Talk yourself into trying.

But here I want to focus on the possibility of you persuading yourself. Before an attempt, talk yourself into it with a self-statement like this:

> 'I expect to feel anxious when I give this a try, and I would feel disappointed if it doesn't work, but I can cope with those feelings. I won't tell myself I shouldn't feel anxious — that's only normal — but I won't exaggerate my anxiety by worrying about how I will go — that's only self-defeating. Now, make sure I have made all reasonable preparation, then give myself a shove and try it!'

During an attempt you can use shorter, less distracting self-instructions to keep up your self-efficacy, such as:
'Good try! Keep it up!'
'Going fine. Keep going.'
'I *can* do it, if I just keep trying.'
What self-instructions would help you to keep trying? In particular, what can you say to yourself to keep at the tasks *you* wish to tackle?

No. 7 tip for motivation Don't think it's a catastrophe when things go wrong.

Having talked yourself into trying, don't talk yourself out of it at the first sign of a problem. In tackling any worthwhile task you may experience a number of setbacks before your eventual success, providing you keep trying. Watch your self-talk for signs of exaggeration: 'Oh, oh. I just made a mistake. That's the end. I knew I could never do this. Nothing works out for me. This will mean the end of my job/marriage/sports career/the world.'

Use a coping self-statement instead: 'I expect to feel disappointed if I make a mistake, and I will feel bad if this whole try does not work, but I can cope with feeling disappointed or bad, and the chance of having those feelings is not a good enough reason for me to throw away my chance of success prematurely. Now, pause and think: what went wrong? How do I fix it, or retrieve the situation?' And make some concrete plans to do just that.

If you think you anticipate catastrophe a lot in your self-talk, with the result of lowering your self-efficacy and reducing your effort, you probably need to systematically learn and apply the coping skill for more realistic thinking, mental relaxation.

No. 8 tip for motivation Use your imagination!

Self-talk is not always in words (or similar symbols). In fact, some psychologists who study thinking have concluded that most of it is done in images, in mental pictures of how things, look, sound, feel, and so on. If someone asks you, 'What are you thinking?', you may reply, 'I was thinking about my next job.' Because you reply in words, there is the impression you were thinking in words, but it's quite likely you were actually thinking in images, imagining the sights and sounds of your next job, as you expect them to be.

Many people will run mental movies, of past events, of preferred fantasies (you have no idea how many times I have won a big lottery), and of coming events. Long before the event actually occurs, you may have lived it a number of times in your imagination. The problem is that many people make those horror movies: they imagine all the ways things are going to go wrong, how badly they will handle the event, how catastrophic the results will be, and how awful they are going to feel. By the time they get to the actual event, they are so anxious they do not do as well as they could, and the only script they are carrying in their heads to guide their performance is a failure script.

You can take this natural tendency to imagine how things will turn out, and make it work for you, rather than against you. Just rewrite the script: instead of a horror movie, watch a success movie. Imagine the upcoming event as vividly as you can, and imagine yourself handling it well. Make your script realistic, by imagining yourself using the genuinely appropriate skills, whether they are task-related or interpersonal. Don't make it unrealistically easy: imagine things going wrong and other people reacting badly, and then imagine how you could handle these problems successfully. By the time the real event rolls along, you will feel more confident and the script you will be carrying in your head to guide your performance will be a success script. Don't underestimate the motivational potential of this technique of imagined rehearsal of success. The US Olympic ski and gymnastics teams, some well-known yacht crews and football teams have all used psychologists as coaches, employing imagined rehearsal of success to build winning motivation, including the motivation to keep going and cope when something goes wrong. Clinical psychologists have used the same technique to get people started on being more assertive and communicative, and to tackle all sorts of tasks they were anxious about. Once you can imagine yourself doing it successfully, give yourself a shove in the back and try it in the real world.

Building self-efficacy by managing arousal

I have already explained that stress is a normal and necessary part of being alive. You need enough arousal to get you going, or you will be a slug, but not so much that you are over-hyped and over-stretched, feeling unable to cope with your present demands, let alone any new ones.

No. 9 tip for motivation   Learn to relax, both mentally and physically.

Relaxation is an active skill, not an absence of activity. Mental relaxation rests on thinking realistically, so your reactions are not exaggerated, in duration or intensity. Physical relaxation involves reducing muscle tension and other physical indications of your stress level, such as your heart rate or blood pressure. It is a useful back-up, but no substitute, for mental relaxation.

But in Chapter 3 I raised with you the possibility that you may have a general problem with stress. If that is so, it will forever be reducing your self-efficacy, lowering your motivation, and so reducing your chances of experiencing success. This, of course, will probably result in further stress. If you have not already done so, I encourage you now to complete the stress self-assessments in Chapter 3 and, if your results do indicate a stress problem, begin a systematic stress-management programme not only for your health's sake, but as a builder of self-efficacy and so of motivation.

7| SUCCESS AND MOTIVATION AT WORK AND PLAY

You may be wondering why I have lumped work and play into the one chapter. Aren't they supposedly opposites? Don't you do one in order to be able to afford to do the other? Well, of course, they do differ in some important ways. You usually get paid for work but pay to play. That is, unless you work as a home-maker or volunteer, in which case you don't get paid, or unless you work at a professional sport, in which case you get paid to play. So the pay distinction is not perfect. Well, you usually work to earn your living, while you play for recreation and relaxation. That's a bit better but, for the purposes of achieving success and building motivation, I suggest work and play are similar in a basic way: they are both about achievement.

In work, you are generally trying to achieve a number of goals: to make a product, to sell something, to provide a service, as well as goals such as earning your wages, commission or profit, perhaps gaining a promotion. In much of play you are also trying to achieve goals: to beat your opponent, to master or improve skills, to earn an award of proficiency, as well as goals such as enjoying yourself, enhancing your relationships, or getting satisfaction from the application of your play skills. Most, if not all, of the behaviour at work and at play is *purposeful*, intended to achieve one or more goals. Even if your play consists of lying on the beach, you could be aiming to achieve some relaxation, a suntan, some entertainment from the novel you are reading or some titillation from the people you are watching.

Indeed, it was the apparent purposefulness of much behaviour that originally led psychologists to propose the motivational theories discussed in the previous chapter. Although the old theories turned out to be of little explanatory value, there is a link: motivation needs goals. To build motivation at work and play, to increase your chances of achieving the realistic success of your personal best, you need to set goals.

Why set goals?

I believe one of the hallmarks of maturity is that your behaviour becomes increasingly self-directed. As children, we need a fair degree of guidance to know what to do and how to do it successfully, and we are very dependent on the praise and approval of others to know we have been successful, a point I will consider further in Chapter 9. If we are growing up successfully, we gradually take over those roles for ourselves, becoming increasingly self-directed and self-rewarded. A realistic approach to self-award I have discussed at length in Chapter 3. Self-direction means setting your own goals.

If your goals are set for you by other people, you are a little robot, submissively fulfilling their wants, not necessarily your own. You may be well aware of this, and feel resentment towards them and a loss of esteem in yourself, both because of your submission and because of the apparently low opinion they have of your ability to participate in setting your own goals. None of this is going to do much for your motivation.

If you have no goals (a practice I was amazed to hear suggested by one of the seminar stars recently), you literally don't know where you are going, other than where other people tell you to go. The pop psychologists have recently been making a fuss about the 'mid-life crisis'. As usual with pop psychology, their discussions have been over-simple — humans go through a number of important life transitions, none of which is more important than the others — and lacking in practical advice. One man came to see me after reading one of these books and said, 'It was just me. It described me exactly.' 'That must have been reassuring,' I replied, 'was it helpful?' He looked honestly puzzled at this question, thought a bit and then said, 'No, but it described me well.'

In my experience, the essence of the 'mid-life crisis' is a lack of acceptable, useful goals. Often it is precipitated by the sufferer having finally accepted the unreality or inappropriateness of some of the goals he started with. As a young adult, it may have seemed a good idea and a feasible one, to be the president of the corporation or the best salesperson in the world or whatever. Twenty years down the track it has become clear he's not going to do it. Although, as we discussed in Chapter 3, he may in fact have realistically been quite successful, he may see the abandoning of these impossible goals as some sign of failure, so down go his self-efficacy and motivation. More problematic, he then has trouble deciding what goals to put in their place. If life isn't all about beating everybody else, what is it about? Salt may be rubbed in these wounds by the emptiness of the marriage and the family or friendships he has meglected all of this time, but his major problem is goal-lessness. Being goal-less is like being a rudderless boat: you may just as well switch off the engine or pull down the sails because, no matter how fast you may be able to go, you aren't really going anywhere. And that's how the mid-life crisis feels. You may need to attend to those neglected relationships and the rest of your balanced lifestyle to overcome this 'crisis', but mostly you need to set some new goals.

None of us lives in a vacuum, uninfluenced by outside factors or pressures, so self-direction is a matter of degree and can be more complex than first appears. The adolescent who feels he must do the opposite to his parents' wishes to 'prove' his independence, has in fact exercised little self-direction compared to what he might have done had he considered all possibilities and chosen the one that really suited him, regardless of how closely it matched his parents' wishes. Similarly, the woman who accepts the strict orders of her authoritarian boss may seem to be exercising little self-direction but in fact she has directed herself to acquiesce, for her own reasons, ranging from simply agreeing with the boss to wanting to keep her job. Self-direction depends as much on the appropriateness of the goal for you, as it does on where the goal originated, a point I will expand shortly.

This does not mean the source of the goal is unimportant. There is no doubt that you will work harder to achieve a goal you feel you had a significant role in setting. On the other hand, people are less motivated towards goals that they see as being imposed on them, even if the goals may seem appropriate. The practical implications of this are two: have as much say as you can in the setting of your goals, and give others as much say as you can in setting goals you expect of them. Later in this chapter I'll explain how to do that.

Goal-setting is important to motivation for a couple of other reasons as well. First, if you are clever enough to set realistic goals, including sub-goals along the way to major but distant goals, you can benefit from a psychological phenomenon called the 'end spurt'. As you approach a goal, you will usually work harder towards it. Many of us start out on a project with enthusiasm, but by the middle, especially if it's a long middle, enthusiasm can flag. Then when you finally see the goal looming over the horizon, your motivation picks up and you finish in a flurry. Clever goal-setting can give you plenty of end spurts.

Second, goals can act as signposts and facilitate your problem-solving. Have you ever been lost at an intersection, wondering which way to go and how far it is? Goals can tell you both. When you are trying to solve problems, at work or play or elsewhere in your life, particularly problems of choice, goals can tell you which way to go because you have already decided where you are going. A goal can also tell you how far you have to go. Goals can be benchmarks to measure your progress against. Whether your goal is to increase your earnings by 10 per cent next year, or reduce your golf handicap by three strokes, or lose 2 kilos of excess weight, a clearly expressed goal allows you to be certain of your progress and so build your motivation.

In sum, setting goals increases the degree of self-directedness of your behaviour, protects you from goal-lessness, improves your problem-solving, and boosts your motivation in several important ways. To achieve all this, you need to go about your goal-setting thoughtfully.

Useful and usable goals

I define a goal as something you intend to achieve by your actions. If you have an idea of something you would like but you cannot specify the actions you will take to achieve it, it's probably only a *wish* or a *dream*. There's nothing wrong with having some wishes or dreams. They can be pleasant for occasional daydreaming or, better still, they may be the starting point for you to formulate some goals. Too much wishing and dreaming, however, could be just the expression of a low self-efficacy: 'I wish things were different, but I don't think I am able to change them.' Enjoy your dreams and wishes but, if they seem important to you, turn them into goals.

You may start by daydreaming of yourself as a good tennis player. That dream could become a goal, like: 'I plan to be selected for our local B grade tennis team this year, by having a lesson each week and practising for at least one hour twice a week.' That's a goal: a clear plan for concrete actions that you intend to take.

Or you may wish you earned more money. That wish could

become a goal, like: 'I intend to earn an extra £5,000 next year by going to college at night to upgrade my qualifications and getting a promotion to supervisor.' Again, that's a clear plan for concrete actions.

The second important characteristic of useful and usable goals is that they are realistic. You may have expected that by now, given our earlier discussions of the need to set realistic goals, but it's worth emphasizing. Unrealistic goals set you up for apparent 'failure' when, in fact, you may have done your realistic best. Take account of what your relevant abilities seem to be, take account of your relevant past experiences and your present life situation, and then set realistic goals. Don't be afraid of limiting yourself unnecessarily by aiming too low. If you achieve any goal easily, you can always use it as a stepping stone and set another one a bit higher. In the meantime, your self-efficacy and motivation will have benefited from the success of achieving that goal.

A point to watch in setting your goals realistically is the degree to which your achievement of them will depend on the behaviour of others. Setting goals which can be sabotaged by the opposition or indifference of others is setting yourself up for an apparent 'failure' when in fact your contribution may have been your realistic best and may deserve to be regarded as a success. Don't set out single-handed to improve a business that employs other people or a relationship which obviously involves other people. Do set out to improve your contribution to such joint enterprises. Later in this chapter I'll be considering how you can most effectively influence the motivation and success rates of others, but you don't do it by accepting responsibility for their behaviour.

Third, almost as an extension of the need for realistic goals, you need goals that can be achieved reasonably soon. I remember rowing for my school (yes, it was a competitive sport and I did enjoy it). In those days we raced over a mile and it was always the third quarter of a mile that was hardest. By then you had used a lot of your energy reserves, you were breathing and working hard, and the finish seemed a long way off. Into the last quarter, with the finish in sight, and it was amazing how much extra energy you could suddenly summon up. I didn't know the phrase, then, but we were enjoying the end spurt and so can you, if you choose goals that are 'in sight'. If you can realistically set a goal that is 'out of sight', in the sense that it will take you some while to achieve it, then you should consider setting sub-goals along the way and focusing on the achievement of each in turn. This will give you the benefit of plenty of end spurts and successes. For example, the goal above of earning an extra £5,000 'next year' is at least twelve months off and your motivation may flag along the way. You can reduce this risk by setting sub-goals, such as: 1 get information about available courses; 2 enrol in the most appropriate course; 3 the course itself may offer a number of sub-goals in the form of assignments; 4 apply for my promotion; and so on.

Fourth, your goals will be more effective motivators if they express *your* interests. This might seem obvious but you could be surprised by the number of people who are struggling to motivate themselves towards goals they are not really interested in. I recently had my first consultation with a woman whose stress is ruining her, her marriage and her family. She is a qualified medical specialist, much in demand amongst other medical specialists for her services. To an outside observer, she seems very successful; in her own eyes, she sees herself as inadequate to her work, which she therefore finds very stressful. As you might guess, central to her problems are a low self-efficacy and unrealistic performance standards. How did she wind up in this situation? Simple: she never wanted to be a doctor. Her interests lay in art, design and music but, when her father ceased to support the family, they in turn expected her to provide the support. So the pressure was on to go into a well-paid profession and today, here she is, a highly qualified, highly stressed person with no motivation towards her work.

Her case may be an extreme example of setting goals that do not reflect your interests, and the anti-motivational consequences, but it is only unusual in terms of degree. Two points in life where many of us are at risk of accepting goals that do not represent our own interests are selecting which subjects to study at senior secondary level, and selecting post-secondary education, training or work. If it's you making the selection, take your time to find out about the long-term implications of going down a particular career path. What is it really like to do that sort of job, day in and day out? Don't be afraid to postpone decisions or to revise them, if they look wrong. Be aware of the probable fact that your advisers, parents or teachers, however well-intended, will be expressing their interests and aspirations, not necessarily yours. If you are the adviser and you genuinely want this child to be a real success, back off and let her choose for herself. If she makes one or two mistakes, if she even winds up spending an extra year getting into a career track that really expresses her interests, the motivational (and other) advantages will far outweigh the costs.

The fifth characteristic of useful and usable goals is that they conform with your values, your notions of what is right and wrong.

This is an important prerequisite because your motivation will be, at best, very mixed if a goal requires you to behave in ways that are very contrary to your values. The goal may attract you, but the behaviour required to achieve it could leave you feeling very guilty, ashamed or unworthy. These bad feelings may not only cancel out the success of the goal but do further damage to your self-image.

Humans can cope with a certain amount of discrepancy between their behaviour and their attitudes, or at least their stated attitudes. In our jargon, a mismatch between the two creates cognitive dissonance: you are aware that you are doing something you see as wrong. Cognitive dissonance makes you feel uncomfortable so you are then likely to act in ways that resolve or at least reduce that mismatch. For example, smokers tend to avoid factual information about the health-damaging effects of smoking, because acknowledging that information creates cognitive dissonance with their smoking behaviour. But there are limits to our ability to resolve cognitive dissonance, and setting goals that are badly mismatched with your values will probably exceed your ability to resolve them and give you very mixed motivation.

As a personal example, I was recently asked to be the guest speaker at a meeting promoting a multi-level selling scheme. I wasn't too sure about multi-level selling, so I rang the Consumer Affairs Bureau to ask if they had heard of it. Their advice was that multi-level selling, while technically legal under the existing law, was effectively no different from pyramid selling, which the state sees as illegal and I certainly see as unethical. I declined the invitation, explaining to the organizer that I was the wrong speaker for them because I would have mixed motivation. He took some personal affront at this implied attack on his integrity and hasn't spoken to me since, which probably makes us both more comfortable. If he had thought about my refusal instead of getting on his high horse, he would have realized I was doing the right thing by him. By not accepting a goal that would have been mismatched with my values, I saved him and his meeting from an unmotivated and unsuccessful performance on my part. Do yourself the same favour: keep your goals in conformity with your values and protect your motivation and successes.

Let's set some goals

If you have not made a practice of systematically setting goals, you will probably find your first attempt a bit time-consuming and hesitant. Stick at it; like any new skill, you will improve with practice, and from now on you should get plenty of that. Goal-setting is a skill for successful living, not a once-only exercise. Achieving goals can mean new ones are needed. Changes in your life situation, skills, interests or values can mean revision of existing goals. Without it becoming a time-wasting obsession, goal-setting deserves your regular attention.

In the table opposite I have listed possible areas in your life, for which you could set goals. These are the areas that apply to most people but I have made provision in the 'Other' category for any area that is important in your life, not covered by the seven I have listed. For example, here you might include 'retirement', a life area that definitely deserves some judicious goal-setting long before it actually arrives.

The second column is 'wants', your wishes or dreams. These may be vague, like 'I would like more friends', or negative, like 'I want to stop drinking too much'. At this stage you are looking only for ideas, for general directions, so almost any possibility will do. You might well benefit from doing a private brainstorming exercise, along the lines set out in Chapter 5. To tap into your creativity and come up with elegant goals you might otherwise never have imagined, stick to the rules for brainstorming. Your sole aim, at this stage, is to think of as many wants, dreams and wishes as you can. Don't leave any out because you think they are impossible, unrealistic or whatever. The weeding out occurs at the next stage and in the meantime an impossible idea, although it may be discarded later, might prompt you to think of a really good, quite practical idea that you would otherwise not have imagined. You can get further ideas for career goals by looking at the positions vacant advertisements in major papers and the possible promotion pathways within your present workplace, for family goals and friendship goals by talking with family and friends, for learning and educational goals by obtaining information from education institutions and adult education programmes. Ideas for personal development may spring more from present dissatisfactions with yourself, such as a wish to be less aggressive and more assertive or a desire to be less shy and more socially at ease.

Once you have identified what you see as your current wants, you begin to turn those into goals. There may well not be enough room to do all of these in the table and, in any case, you will need to revise them from time to time, so you could do your actual goal-setting on a separate sheet of paper for each life area. In line with the discussion above, you should now be setting goals that are

GOAL-SETTING

POSSIBLE LIFE AREAS	WANTS (May be vague)	GOALS (Must be realistic, interesting, comfortable, clear and feasible outcomes)
1 Career	_____	_____
2 Family	_____	_____
3 Friends	_____	_____
4 Learning/education .	_____	_____
5 Recreation	_____	_____
6 Health	_____	_____
7 Personal development	_____	_____
8 Others (e.g. retirement?) ...	_____	_____

realistic, interesting to you, compatible with your values, clear and actionable. Each goal needs to be expressed in terms of an outcome, not the process involved in obtaining the outcome. Instead of something like, 'I want to improve my computer skills', you would say, 'I want to be able to write my own computer programmes for my business applications.' The point is that *you need a clear indicator of when each goal has been achieved.* You may be improving your computer skills steadily, but you will only know you have achieved this goal when your improvement allows you to perform at the level you have specified, writing your own programmes. Without clearly specified outcomes for your goals, you cannot tell when you have achieved them. This specification may be difficult, at first, because you began with just a vague wish, like 'to improve my computer skills', but it is essential. What exactly would you eventually be doing that shows you have achieved your goal? If someone else was to judge your goal achievement, what would you tell her to look for as a visible indication that you had made it? If you were judging someone else aiming for the same goal, what would you look for in his behaviour that would clearly indicate he had achieved the goal?

'But,' you may be thinking, 'I want to improve my computer skills (or meet whatever want you began with) in more ways than just that one. I also want to be able to use a word-processing programme to write my reports, and I want to be able to use a spread-sheet programme to do the financial side of those reports.' Fine, those two sound like good outcomes for goal-setting, too. One want may generate many goals. The order in which you address those goals may be dictated by some of them depending on your prior achievement of others. Or you may need to put them in order of priority, in terms of their urgency, importance and accessibility, as I discussed in Chapter 3 in the context of establishing a balanced lifestyle. And achieving one goal that meets part of a want may lead you to set another goal in the same area. For example, you are unlikely ever to stop wanting to enjoy good health, but you may forever be setting, achieving, replacing and revising goals to satisfy that want. As a part of specifying the outcome in a goal, you may choose to set a target date by which you intend to have achieved that goal. Setting realistic target dates as a part of your goals, when that's appropriate, can help you to pace yourself and boost your motivation.

Having specified clearly the outcome of your goal, you also need to specify what you will do to achieve that outcome if your goal is to be actionable. For example, your goal may now become, 'I will attend the business computers course at my local college, so that I am able to write my own programmes for my business.' Now, that's a useful and usable goal that spells out exactly what you are going to do, with a clearly identifiable outcome to signal your successful achievement.

Some goals may involve essentially one step, such as completing the computer course at your local college in the example above. But some may require a number of steps, together or sequentially, for their final achievement. So spelling out these goals requires you to write a *plan of action*, a series of concrete behaviours you plan to do. Naturally it's possible that the outcome of any one step may cause you to revise the later steps in your plan and that's where the signposting aspect of goals will be helpful. When an unexpected problem does turn up, you will solve it better because you know where you are going. It can also help to try to anticipate those problems. Imagine yourself working through your plan a step at a time. What obstacles can you already anticipate? What steps can you plan now to handle those obstacles if they arise? A problem you have predicted and prepared for is still a problem, and tackling it will still slow your progress somewhat. But it will not have the dismaying effect on your motivation and self-efficacy of an unforeseen problem with no immediately apparent solution. You cannot predict every obstacle to your goals but you can do some successful problem prediction and appropriate preparation.

If you are going to avoid the trap of turning this book into an entertaining seminar for one, you need to be acting on any suggestions that are appropriate for you. If you have not already done a systematic goal-setting exercise, I strongly encourage you to take a break from reading soon, and set some goals. Doing that exercise properly, as I have explained it, should build your motivation and get you implementing some of your plans. But it is possible that, no matter how attractive the goal is, some of your plans can be unattractive in themselves. For example, your goal of getting a promotion at work at the end of the year may involve your studying certain material that you don't particularly enjoy. You can see it will be of some help on the job and you believe it is not ignoring your interests too much to master the stuff, but you expect to find it difficult to motivate yourself to stick to your study plans. You need some motivational help.

Contracting: your motivational aid

I have previously made the point that intrinsic motivation — you directing and approving your own self-satisfying behaviour — is more effective than extrinsic motivation — someone else setting your goals and offering you a reward for achieving them. That's true, but it does not mean we are not influenced by extrinsic rewards, especially if they are rewards of your choice to be earned by behaviours of your choice. Contracting may initially look like a retreat to extrinsic motivation but it is, in fact, a way of strengthening self-directedness. This is especially true with children, as I'll explain in Chapter 9, but for now let's focus on how you can use it as a motivational aid.

Any contracts you have been involved with previously were probably agreements between people for the delivery of certain goods or services in exchange for certain payments. In contrast, a motivational contract is an agreement you make with yourself for the delivery of certain behaviours (to achieve your goal) in exchange for certain rewards. Don't underestimate the motivational boost you can obtain from a well-designed contract. Contracts are particularly helpful to keep you motivated to stick to a plan you know is in your own best interests, but that you expect to find difficult or not immediately rewarding in itself. The study example above is a good one: obtaining the qualification and being eligible for the promotion will both be enjoyable successes and towards the end of the course you may well get the added boost of an end spurt. But making yourself settle down to enough study during the middle of the course can require some real motivation, especially if you don't find the coursework itself very rewarding. Then a contract can be a helpful motivational aid. I have set out an example of a contract for this situation on page 111.

You can follow the same layout in writing your own motivational contracts. Specify clearly the outcome required by the contract; make it for observable, measurable behaviours. If it's unobservable or vague, you cannot tell when your contract has been kept. Identify appropriate rewards for yourself: what do you want enough to help you stick to your contract? Rewards can be material, a gift of some sort for yourself, or behaviours, either allowing yourself access to an activity you enjoy or a pleasant behaviour given to you by a supportive spouse or friend, like a back rub or whatever you fancy. Cash makes quite a good reward. Open a special purpose, 'contract' account and each occasion or each week that you stick to your contract reward yourself by depositing a sum that is meaningful and affordable to you. You can use the accumulated funds to give yourself a grand reward for sticking to your contract for three months or for achieving the end goal, like passing your computer course.

Penalties can act as a further motivational incentive, so add them to your contract. Suitable penalties might be doing disliked

AN EXAMPLE OF A CONTRACT

TO ACHIEVE MY GOAL of being eligible for promotion at work by the end of this year, I plan to attend the travel agents' course at my local college.

Each week that I go to classes and complete any reading or assignments set that week, I will reward myself by going to the club with my friends on Saturday afternoon and paying £5 into my goal account.

Any week that I miss a class or don't do any set reading or assignment, without a genuinely good excuse, my penalty is to mow the lawn on Saturday afternoon and donate £5 to the Crippled Cockroaches' Home.

I realize that this contract is an aid to my motivation, to help me achieve a goal I want but expect to find difficult so, if I cheat on this contract, I only cheat myself.

Date .... Signed ....
(A supportive spouse or friend can witness your contract, if you want, and be the person you report your progress to.)

chores (e.g. washing the car, mowing the lawn, cleaning out the cupboards) whether they need doing or not, or losing access to a preferred activity. If you are using cash as a reward, you can use loss of cash as a penalty. Write out a cheque for the amount you are using as a reward, make it payable to a charity you hate, loathe and despise, sign it but don't date it. I suggest you pin up your contract somewhere suitable, as a visual prompt to your motivation, and you can pin the cheque up next to it for the same purpose. Any occasion or week that you don't keep your contract, without a *genuinely* good reason, date the cheque and post it off to the charity. By selecting a charity, the money goes to a 'good' cause but no one in your immediate environment stands to gain from your breaking your contract. By selecting a charity you dislike, you increase your incentive level considerably because, if you do have to post them your cheque, they not only get your hard-earned money but they also get your name to pester for future donations.

The common objections to contracting as a motivational aid are that it is 'artificial', that it represents 'a lack of willpower, a sign of weakness', and that it is tantamount to 'bribery'. Let's deal with these objections quickly. Contracting certainly is artificial; so are large slabs of your environment, including many anti-motivational factors. Contracting is a way of restructuring part of your environment so that it supports your motivation. Far from being a sign of weakness, I think making appropriate use of contracting is a sign of strength in being able to use appropriate living skills. It seems far more weak, to me, to be aware of a potentially helpful procedure, like contracting, but to ignore it out of a fear of being seen as weak.

I commend contracting to you as a motivational aid, particularly for sticking to longer plans with less intrinsic rewards along the way. Are there some contracts you could be using right now, in light of the goals you just set? If so, take the time to write your contracts now and start using them. Don't be afraid to adjust a contract so that it is as helpful as possible. It's not unusual to set your performance standard, or your rewards or penalties, too high or too low to begin with. Or you may wish to keep raising your performance standard towards an eventual goal performance. Adjust the components of your contract up or down, until the contract works for you, then use it for as long as you feel you need that motivational aid. And then discard it, giving yourself a pat on the back for successful use of appropriate skills.

Looking successful

In the interests of openness in communication, let me admit I have trouble with this topic. I have a strong abhorrence for the superficial, the phony show with no substance underneath. The brochure for one American course on improving your image, after shyly admitting it 'could be one of the most important turning points in your career', goes on to promise that participants will be taught how to 'convey poise, sincerity and authority'. You will note that the organizers don't enquire whether you actually have or offer to help you acquire these qualities; they simply plan to show you how to 'convey' them. That sort of phony show is well out of step with my values, so it is not one of my goals for this book to encourage you to put on false fronts.

On the other hand, it is irrefutable that superficial impressions, especially first impressions, do count and indeed count a lot. Researchers have repeatedly found that people do make all sorts of judgements and assumptions about other people, solely on the basis of appearance. Further, they have found that first impressions, once made, are very durable; later evidence that contradicts a first impression may well be disregarded as 'out of character'. It may be expected that better looking applicants are more likely to get jobs, but it has also been observed that better looking candidates get more votes in elections, that better looking students are given higher grades, that better looking people receive preferential treatment in a number of ways. There is neither logic nor justice to it, but it happens.

So, in our realistic approach to success, what do we do? I suggest you pay reasonable attention to your appearance and presentation because, whether you like it or not, other people will be judging you on them and reacting to you in terms of those judgements. Beware of the pop psychologists in the image industry who claim to be able to tell you exactly how you should dress, speak, stand, sit and even eat and drink, for instant success. Their authoritative claims have no scientific support and are collections of their own prejudices, however glossily they are decked out. Simple observation of the other people in your spheres of work and play should give you an idea of what is generally seen as acceptable and that should be all the guidance you need. Obviously, if you dress or behave in ways that are very different from most of your fellows, you will be seen as unusual. You will need to decide for yourself whether that would be advantageous, but the truth is that, in many workplaces, it would not. On the other hand, I can't imagine a clearer statement of low self-esteem than feeling you need someone to tell you what to wear or how to comb your hair or what colour your suit should be. Somewhere in there you need to strike a balance between what you feel is expected of you and what feels right for you.

I rarely wear a coat and tie to my office, because it would feel pretentious to me. But I do dress neatly and simply, because people coming to consult with me expect to talk to a professional psychologist and looking like one enhances my influence, making me more helpful. I would dress similarly to deliver a seminar to psychologists or other health professionals, because that would be how many of them would dress, so I don't violate their expectations and lose plausibility. But I probably would wear a coat and tie, perhaps even a suit, to talk to a meeting of business people, because that's how they expect their authority figures to dress, so they pay more attention to what I have to say. I get my hair cut more often these days, because I have chosen to use television to try to influence the psychological habits of the community, and looking neat enhances my influence. But I keep my beard. So, I'm trying to strike that balance between looking right for my current audience and feeling right for myself.

In terms of presentation, there may be quite sensible goals for improvement you could set. If your work involves public speaking or presentations to groups of any sort, you might benefit from some training in presentation skills. Such training is available from commercial organizations and adult education resources, or you might try some self-help through organizations. If your work involves one-to-one interactions, the skills for handling those successfully are in Chapters 4 and 5, and you may like to beef up your self-help by attending a training course in communication, conflict-resolution, assertion or problem-solving. Take this suggestion with a pinch of salt for apparent self-interest, but I would strongly suggest courses conducted by qualified psychologists. I know there are *some* non-psychologists who offer quite good training in some of these areas (I hope they resist the temptation to dabble in therapy when a trainee raises a personal problem), but I cannot suggest how you would identify these good trainers from the many duds beforehand, other than by personal recommendation from someone who has already done their course.

Motivating others to be successful

Throughout most of this book, my focus is on how you can motivate yourself effectively and enjoy realistic success, although in Chapter 9 I will consider at length how you can help your children to be successful. Of course, some readers will also want to motivate others to be successful. Indeed, doing so could be an important part of your personal success as an executive, a manager, a supervisor, a sports coach, or some other sort of leader. So, how do you apply all these ideas to someone other than yourself?

In part, the answer is self-evident: just apply exactly the same ideas and techniques as I have been suggesting you use personally. If you go back and review the Tips for Success and the Tips for Motivation in the first three chapters, it won't take much imagination on your part to turn them into tips for motivating others. It will take much more thoughtful and persistent effort actually to apply them in your leadership role, but that could make a good set of goals for you. You could begin right now collecting all those Tips and rewriting them, as you would apply them to others. Then identify opportunities to start doing that in practice. If necessary, set some goals and work out some plans.

But there is one point I have previously made, so crucial to your ability to motivate others, that I want to spell it out in some detail. You will recall that I suggested that goals are more effective motivators if you were largely responsible for setting them yourself; conversely, goals that you feel you had little role in setting are less effective motivators. The approach to work design in which the boss sets the goals and the workers toe the line is called technocratic. It has been our traditional approach to work design and it has been marked by poor motivation, low productivity, high error and wastage rates, and antagonistic industrial relations. It has not been what I would call a screaming success.

An alternative approach, growing steadily in popularity, is sociotechnical work design. The key difference is participation in goal-setting and more recent studies have shown that the greater the degree of participation, the better the process works. Sociotechnical work design builds and maintains motivation, improves productivity, reduces error and wastage rates, and creates co-operative industrial relations. In the projects I have worked on, and clearly in the abundant research now done on this issue, it is a marked success.

The mechanism for achieving this participation in goal-setting is collaborative decision-making. You can run incentive schemes, or conduct razzmatazz wind-up seminars, or threaten to sack people, but none of it, I repeat, none of it will be as effective as genuine participation in building motivation and achieving lasting success. As the General Electric Company ruefully discovered in their light-fitting factory in Hawthorn, Chicago, doing almost anything can increase motivation temporarily; keeping it up was more elusive. Well, the secret need elude you no longer.

'Why,' you may be thinking, 'if collaborative decision-making is so wonderful, isn't everybody doing it?' I have found several common reasons. First, there are still some managers who just haven't heard about it. Well, now you have. Second, there are some who are opposed to it on ideological grounds, although I think that opposition is often ill-informed. I can't see how increasing profitability is 'creeping socialism'. Still, if it is not consonant with your values, you won't set it as a goal, although you should recognise you are limiting your ability to be a successful leader by that choice. Third, and I think usually the real reason, is fear. Fear of something different, and fear of losing control. Managers and people in authority often suffer from the illusion that they are in control and are frightened of losing that control. As I discussed in the context of assertion, no one really has control over anybody else and often attempts to assert that illusory control have counter-productive effects. All we ever have over others is influence and the great benefit from collaborative decision-making is that it enhances your influence. People will pay more attention to what you have to say within a co-operative framework than they will within an authoritarian and aggressive approach.

Don't assume that the benefits of collaborative decision-making are only for profit-making organizations. They have been equally enjoyed by non-profit organisations and I can see no reason why they would not also be effective in building motivation in sports teams.

So, if you would like to motivate others to be more successful, do systematically apply the principles throughout this book to your dealings with others. But especially invite them to join you in setting shared goals, and you may be amazed at your success as a leader.

8| SUCCESS IN LOVE

Love? What's love doing in a book on success and motivation? Are we going soppy towards the end? Won't the pursuit of love just distract me from the more serious business of being successful and motivated?

If you really did react like that, it's time you went back to Chapter 3 for a refresher on my definition of realistic success. It includes, you will recall, success not only in the careers and recreations of your choice, but also in your social and intimate relationships. The psychologist whose work we will draw upon most, Professor Robert Sternberg of Yale University, had established himself as one of the leading theoreticians and researchers in the field of human intelligence before he began his research into love. When he was asked why he had extended his interests in such a new direction, he replied that in high school he had been told there were only two things in life that matter, brains and sex. 'I spent the first part of my career studying brains,' he said, 'and now along comes sex.' More seriously, he added, love is an understudied topic that is extremely important to people's lives.

And important it is, within my definition of success, within a balanced lifestyle, and within society as the foundation of stable relationships and families. The distress caused by unsuccessful love relationships will do little for anyone's motivation, an observation that can be confirmed by anyone who has watched or participated in the decline of a relationship and its ultimate end in divorce. There is a further ripple effect of this death of love, on friends, associates and family, especially any children of the relationship, who may in turn have their chances of success in love reduced.

So success in love is important, for you, your health and well-being, for your family and friends, for your employer (even if that's you), and for the rest of society. It deserves its balanced share of your attention and effort. And it isn't as understudied as Professor Sternberg may once have suggested. Thanks to his and others' research, we now know a fair bit about what love is, how to find it, and how to keep it.

Such research troubles some people. The romantics amongst us baulk at the idea of studying something like love scientifically. Let me repeat a point I have made before: science is not the only way of studying the universe, and not always the most appropriate way. If you want to know what love *feels* like, you would do much better to read some good poetry or literature or listen to a good love song or watch a good love movie, than to wade through a scientific research report. What science does better than other approaches to the universe is provide testable theories about the nature of things, and usable technologies that have a reasonable chance of working. So if you want to understand the *nature* of love, and you want some *practical suggestions* on how to find it and keep it, a scientific approach will serve you better than a literary or artistic one. A lot better, as you will see.

What is love?

There are a number of different kinds of love, depending on the ages, sexes and relationships of the participants. They are all potentially important and I will try to address them all. Much of the theory I will cover applies to, and even explains some of the differences amongst differents kinds of love. Many of the suggestions I will offer apply, with some commonsense variation, to different kinds of love, although most of what I would advise for making successful relationships with your children I will cover in the next chapter.

Professor Sternberg has proposed that love consists of three components. The presence or absence and comparative strengths of these three components reflect the nature and stage of each love relationship, as well as its potential strong points and problems. So let's consider each in turn.

Intimacy is the emotional component of love. Professor Sternberg defines intimacy as including closeness, sharing, communication and support, the behaviours through which the two people express their emotional interdependence. Emotional intimacy is when you 'like' the other person, maybe a little, maybe a lot. In a peer relationship, intimacy tends to increase steadily at first, as a couple develop trust in each other and share increasingly personal information. Eventually it levels off, ideally at the point of closeness appropriate for the relationship: fairly close for a marriage or special friendship, varyingly distant for other friendships. Parent-child relationships tend to be lop-sided and changing in intimacy. Parents may expect and encourage emotional intimacy from their children while not being willing to show as much in return, and not recognizing their emotional dependence on their children until something threatens the relationship. As the children become teen-agers, they are often less emotionally intimate with their parents, partly as a result of their naturally growing independence but sometimes because they expect their parents to make negative judgements of their attitudes and feelings.

In a long-term adult relationship, emotional intimacy may seem to disappear but be present in a latent form, usually brought out when the couple have to cope with a large problem, such as a death in the family, a prolonged separation or, paradoxically, divorce. Some couples only realize after divorce how close and mutually dependent they were. A real loss of intimacy means the relationship is fading out, that you will like and trust each other less. This could mean you are outgrowing a friendship, or adjusting to a lesser level of intimacy with an adult child, or it could mean you are in a declining marriage.

Passion is the motivational component of love, including physiological arousal and an intense desire to be united with your beloved. It is largely but not exclusively sexual and so, I think, only appropriate in peer relationships. In contrast to emotional intimacy, passion develops quickly. It is the sole component of 'love at first sight', which is why I think the phrase is more accurately rendered as 'lust at first sight'. Under the influence of passion, you feel highly excited by your beloved's presence, you tend to miss her or think about him a lot while apart, and you are inclined to notice only her good points, developing an unrealistically positive view of your beloved as God's gift to humanity, with no faults of any kind. Passion provides the motivation to develop the other two aspects of love in an erotic relationship, both of which need time and certain behaviours to grow.

I think that passion depends a lot on the novelty effect, the excitement of a new relationship, of discovering and exploring someone new, emotionally and physically. Even a couple which develops a passionate relationship after having known each other for some time is looking at each other in a new way and often engaging in new, passionate activities. At this stage you are focusing on only the attractive features of your beloved, intensifying your passion. Why not? It certainly feels excitingly good, and having this demi-god express attraction for you is an added reward for your self-esteem. A key role for novelty within passion would explain why it inevitably fades, as it does, usually from six to thirty months after beginning the relationship. The time needed for passion to fade seems to depend on your ability to spend time with your beloved. The more obstacles to your being together, the longer passion lasts. Move in with each other and you can be over it quickly.

These observations also support my notion that novelty is a key factor behind passion. The more time you have together, the less novel the relationship becomes, the more you notice that your beloved does in fact have a few faults and less attractive features and the more you learn about your ability — or inability — to develop the other two components of love with *this* person. So, unquestioning, blindly enthusiastic passion fades, for everybody. If it disappears, you may still have a good friendship with this person, if that's appropriate to this relationship and your expectations. Otherwise the infatuation and this love affair may be over. If it disappears from a long-term relationship, like your marriage, that will reduce your motivation to look after the relationship and will increase its vulnerability.

Commitment is the cognitive or thinking component of love. It involves the initial choice to become involved with this person, and then the repeated choice to develop and maintain that love relationship by behaving in appropriate ways. Commitment in adult relationships typically begins low, growing gradually at first, reflecting your uncertainty about the future of this new relationship, and then building more quickly as certainty develops. That increasing certainty reflects the growing trust and liking that result from developing emotional intimacy, and from the rewarding nature of passion when that's a part of the relationship. All three are hopefully present in your marriage, while commitment in a friendship or parent-child relationship results from the rewards of successful emotional intimacy. Some parents can maintain a high level of commitment to their relationships with their children, even when these are not very rewarding, although I have seen that wear out in cases of bad parent-adolescent conflict. On their side, some teenagers will lose their commitment to their relationships with their parents if they perceive the relationship as lacking successful emotional intimacy, usually as a result of either neglect or conflict.

Thus a willing commitment depends on the success of the other components of love. Unwilling commitment may result from a sense of obligation to the relationship, or fears of being alone or of the stigma of divorce or broken families, but such relationships are at best mediocre and at worst conflict-ridden and miserable. When the costs of staying in the relationship outweigh the commitment to stay, you have a very fragile relationship.

Recipes for successful relationships

Different kinds of relationships involve different combinations of these three components, and therefore different approaches to be successful. Professor Sternberg has proposed eight different kinds of love relationships, involving the various possible combinations of his three components, but I find his classification confuses sequence and content. Some of his eight kinds of love may well occur sequentially within the one relationship; others would never be appropriate within some of your relationships because of their differing nature. So I will instead talk about five basic types of love relationships, a classification which I think more closely reflects how people experience them: self-love, non-love relationships, platonic relationships, erotic relationships, and adult-child relationships. Adults may well have proper and successful love relationships with children other than their own, but I believe parent-child love relationships are the most important of these, for both the adults and the children, so I will consider these in the next chapter.

Self-love

To have a successful relationship with others, you must have a successful relationship with yourself. Of course, that's what this whole book is about, being realistically successful in your own eyes, and nowhere is that more important than in the area of relationships. If you don't respect yourself, you won't expect others to, so you will slip into being submissive or aggressive. If you don't like yourself, you won't expect others to, so you will be poor company or avoid company altogether. If you don't love yourself, in the sense of seeing yourself as lovable, you won't believe it when someone says to you, 'I love you.' It will go through the filter of your low self-esteem and come out as, 'I want something.' After all, you know they can't *really* love you because you believe that no one could. If you don't see yourself as sexy, in the sense of being reasonably good at giving and receiving sexual pleasure, then you won't act sexy and your negative belief becomes a self-fulfilling prophecy.

Realistic and reasonable self-love is the foundation for your successful love relationships with others, so all of my advice and suggestions for building your self-efficacy are relevant. Now you need to apply them to your self-efficacy for making and keeping successful love relationships. Give yourself *accomplishments* in this area by carefully applying the advice and suggestions following. If you are in failing relationships that are reducing your self-efficacy, improve them or quit them. Make sure you set *realistic goals*, in light of the relationship myths I will debunk later. Look at the *successful models* in relationships around you. *Persuade yourself* to try, with sensible self-talk, like that below, and imagined rehearsal of success. And watch your level of *arousal*, whether generally high stress is interfering with your attempts at relationship success, or trying to develop better relationships is so upsetting for you, that you should get some professional help. Don't neglect the role that successful self-love will play in your being able successfully to share love with others.

Successful single living

It would be a serious misinterpretation of my definition of success in your social and intimate relationships if you assumed I meant you must be in a couple relationship. Although the predominant expectation in our society is that adults live in couples and many social activities and institutions are geared to couples, I do not know of any psychological reason why anyone should feel obliged to be coupled. A network of friends is a most desirable resource, a point I will return to. But I can think of no more practical expression of your self-love than your ability to live by yourself successfully. Unfortunately few adults have had the experience of truly independent and autonomous living, and even then often only briefly, between late adolescence or young adulthood and marriage. Many, particularly women, go straight from living dependently with their parents to living dependently with a spouse, burdening their marriages with their over-dependence and rocking the boat later, when they begin to develop some independence.

One of your goals may quite reasonably be a successful marriage. You will prepare yourself better for that if you have first consolidated yourself as an autonomous adult, one able to live with and depend on yourself successully and enjoyably. Then you may choose to be in a couple relationship without the desperation of telling yourself you have to be in it. Or you may cope better if you find yourself single again, for whatever reason. Or you will be more successful at living singly for a part or all of your adult life. More women are pursuing careers first and marriage later, if at all; more people are divorced; more widowed people have independent financial means; and more young people are leaving the parental home earlier; all trends creating more one-person households. Yet there has been little acceptance of training for living as a single adult.

Successful single living requires reasonable mastery of two sets of skills: social skills, for the acquisition and maintenance of a social support group, and self-care skills, to cope with basic tasks that may have been shared, delegated or done for you before.

Successful social skills

By social skills I mean the skills you use to mix successfully with people in social situations, and through which you meet people, and make and build friendships. As such, these are skills for everybody, not just single people. Once people do couple up, they often cut back on other close friendships, which is a sad loss of potential good times and support, further increasing dependence on the couple relationship. Later, in the discussion of erotic relationships, I will point out that a good long-term relationship encourages you to do your own thing away from your partner, as well as sharing good times as a couple. A circle of friends can facilitate those independent activities. Further, if you are looking for a couple relationship and do not wish to live singly, you will still need to start by making friendships, looking for the one that has longer-term potential. So let's all get started.

Finding friends

Finding potential friends seems to be easier for late adolescents and young adults than it is for older adults, because the majority of recognized mixing places are aimed at those younger groups. However, I suggest that difference may be illusory. Other people's expectations of you and a relationship with you will reflect the location of your meeting. Pubs, discos, night clubs, cocktail bars and so on are generally frequented by people looking for brief and casual relationships. If you are looking for a one-night stand, they are the places to be. If you are looking for a more committed relationship, you may find a casual relationship that eventually develops that way, but you should expect some disappointments in your search.

The route I recommend is slower, but much more likely to turn up longer lasting relationships. First, you need to find and begin some recreational activities. They should be activities you enjoy for their own sake (and immediately you are meeting the recreational needs of a successfully balanced life), but through which you can expect to meet new people. A hobby that involves you working alone at home on your personal computer may be good recreation, but is unlikely to help you meet new friends, unless you combined it with going to meetings of a computer users' club.

Stuck for ideas? Daily and local newspapers can contain suggestions, especially the larger ones that have a weekly guide to activities in your town. They generally list all sorts of activities and groups, indoors and outdoors, one-off and regular, sporting, artistic, political, scientific and other special interests. Read through and circle anything that sounds interesting. It helps to approach this exercise in a brainstorming frame of mind: don't leave anything out for practical or cost reasons, circle everything that looks interesting to you. Even if you later have to discard an idea, for whatever reason, it may have prompted another, quite usable idea that you would otherwise not have had. Another excellent path for meeting people is adult education courses. They can range from one-off seminars, to summer schools or full-year courses, covering a galaxy of topics, from the very mundane to the esoteric.

I have to report that specifically singles' organizations have a mixed record of success as meeting places. Every time I say this I get shouted at by one or two singles' clubs, and I am sure that some of them work reasonably well some of the time at helping some of their members make new friendships. But I have often been told by people who have tried singles' clubs that they can be marred by an air of desperation, that attending one felt like being on inspection in a meat market. I suggest you treat them as you would any new activity: try one or two, if you want to, and if you do enjoy their activities and make some new friends, great! If not, discard them and try something else from your list of possible social activities.

Introduce yourself

The big advantage to meeting people through sharing enjoyable activities is that you already have at least one common interest that provides some of your conversation and good times together, beginning the process of building intimacy. The disadvantage is that people are going to the activity to do it, not primarily to meet people. Even if they are there with both recreational and social intentions, like you, they may also be a bit shy (like you?). Either way, you will have to take more responsibility for initiating social contact than you might need to in a purely social setting. This is where you will need to use some basic social skills.

For all of these skills, there is an important component of *non-verbal behaviour*. You will recall from our discussion of communication back in Chapter 4, that most of your emotional impact on another person is conveyed by your non-verbal behaviour, rather than by what you say. This is certainly true of social situations. If you look tense or shy, you are quite likely to trigger similar feelings in the person you are talking with. On the other hand, if you look reasonably relaxed and comfortable that helps to put the other person at ease and facilitates your conversation. Try to keep *eye contact*, about half of the time. Either too little or too much can be off-putting. If you find eye contact difficult, look at a spot in the middle of the other person's forehead, instead. Try to *smile* at appropriate times, such as when you first meet or if something funny is being discussed. Smiling makes you look friendly. Make sure you *speak audibly*, loudly and clearly enough to be understood, without coming on too strong. Finally, use a few relaxed *hand gestures* to animate your conversation, without imitating a windmill.

To start a conversation, just introduce yourself: 'Hallo, my name's Bob. What's yours?' You don't need anything more elaborate than that. Try to ask mostly *open-ended questions*. These are questions that leave most of the answer open to the other person, such as: 'What do you do in your spare time?' Closed-ended ques-

THE MYTHS OF FRIENDSHIP

1   Lovers are better than friends.

Well, that depends on what you had in mind. Lovers are probably better and more appropriate for sharing your passion with, but good friends can be at least equally good for sharing intimacy.

2   Friendship should happen naturally.

I am coming to loathe the word, 'natural', which I assume should mean free of unusual influence but is usually used to mean 'habitual' or 'unthinking', neither of which I see as guarantees of success. You may eventually be habitually good at making successful love relationships, but that will take a lot of deliberate practice and even then require continuing effort. That's what commitment is about.

3   Single people should have single friends.

Or so some couples seem to believe, since they never invite their single friends home. Security for your relationships depends on their success, not on hiding them from 'threats'. People should have friends.

4   Close friends must be of the same sex

Or we'll all be suspicious. Given Kinsey's discovery of how many people have homosexual feelings and the sizeable minority who have had at least transient homosexual relations, this myth is really silly. Very successful and valuable friendships may involve good intimacy and strong commitment, without any significant passion. Even when some passionate feelings occur, you can choose to accept them without having to express them. This myth just cheats you of half the population as potential friends.

5   Best friends are the only worthwhile kind.

Again it depends on what you had in mind. Best friends are important for intimacy and support. Casual friends can be at least equally good for sharing recreations and enjoying fun. Some of them may eventually become better friends.

6   Friends are always there.

Or they weren't 'real' friends. That's a good example of black and white thinking. If your friends are also trying to lead a balanced lifestyle, then there will inevitably be times when they are not available to you, which is why you should have more than one, rather than putting such unreasonable demands on someone.

---

tions give the other person little choice as to how he will answer, such as: 'Do you go fishing?' He can really only answer 'Yes' or 'No', so he isn't contributing much to the conversation. Open-ended questions give the other person an invitation to say as much as she wants, which takes the conversational load off you. Closed-ended questions make assumptions about the other person, and may reflect your interests more than his. Open-ended questions show an interest in finding out what this person is actually like, rather than you putting your assumptions or interests on to her. Work out a few and have them up your mental sleeve, ready to use, like: 'What sort of work do you do?' or 'How do you fill in a typical day?' or 'What are your hobbies or interests?'

When it seems appropriate, *give compliments*, meaning a clear statement of what you liked, such as: 'That's a great outfit you're wearing. It really suits you.' Or, 'That was a good restaurant you chose. I enjoyed that dinner, especially your company.' People like to be liked and are then more likely to like you back. Don't go overboard and lay it on too thickly, or your compliments will seem unimportant, but do deliberately remark on the points in your friend or relationship that you especially like. On the other side of the coin, *accept compliments* clearly and non-defensively, such as: 'Thanks, I'm glad you liked it.' Or, 'Yes, that was fun. Let's do it again soon.' Do *not* throw compliments back into your friend's face by being defensive, such as: 'Oh, it's just a bunch of rags I picked up at a sale.' Or, 'Yes, I suppose it was okay but I only got the name of the place from the Good Food Guide' (ignoring your friend's compliment about your enjoyable company).

Ignoring or belittling compliments punishes the other person for trying to be friendly towards you. Accepting compliments does not mean you have a swelled head, only that you are capable of being friendly.

During all your social conversations, *accept silences* as a normal event. Comfortable conversation has a relaxed pace, which may well include periods of silence. People often go silent because they are thinking about something. If you want to hear what *he* thinks, rather than what you expect him to think, accept the silence of his thinking period. Don't imagine you are a human radio station with an obligation to fill all the available time with some sort of noise, however trite. If you think you have both genuinely run out of conversation, relax, take your time, and pick another open-ended question or topic from your mental list of possibilities.

Watch your self-talk!

Beware of mind-reading, of assuming that the other person is judging you badly or does not like you, when you almost certainly do not have any evidence to confirm that assumption. Unless she actually turns around and says to your face, 'You are the most boring and ugly twit I've ever met,' you don't really know what she's thinking. The pained look on his face may come from a toothache, or the silence may result from her shyness. If you want to clarify the situation, use some good communication, à la Chapter 4.

Throughout the process of making friends, beware of the influence of popular myths about friendships, attitudes that could interfere with your success in relationships. I have discussed these in the table on page 126 and I recommend you consider them now.

There are three common mistakes in thinking that could hold you back in making friendships. The first is to think something like: 'I can't get into relationships because my last one ended.' This is an example of the common thinking mistake of *over-generalizing*, assuming that because something happened to you once or twice, it will always be like that. In the real world, situations are rarely that simple or repetitive. The second is to think something like: 'No one could really like *me*, because I am so ugly, dull, boring' (or whatever). Once again you see what a key role your self-esteem plays in success in relationships, and so how important it is to build a realistic and robust self-image. Do be willing to look at yourself realistically. Should you improve your appearance? Do you try too hard to impress? Are you too passive, too self-devaluing, or too aloof? Realistic self-esteem can pinpoint goals for improvement. The third mistake is to think something like: 'If I try to make friends (again), I will only be rejected and that will hurt too much (again), so it's safer not to try.' This is an example of the common thinking mistake of *imagining the worst*, meaning to expect things to turn out very badly when there is no reason why they should necessarily do so. If you catch yourself using self-talk like any of these three mistakes, you should deliberately replace it with a coping self-statement, like this:

'I expect to feel anxious mixing with people and trying to make friends. I would feel bad if I made a social mistake, or was rejected by someone. But I can cope with those feelings, and the chance of them happening is not a good enough reason for me to miss out on friendships or wind up lonely. So, choose whom I will talk to, work out what I will say to start . . . now, do it!' And give yourself a shove in the back and get going.

Let me draw to your attention the emotional trade-off in this self-statement. You are telling yourself to accept some anxiety and maybe occasional embarrassment or hurt for the chance of feeling good in successful relationships. The self-defeating trap many shy people fall into is to protect themselves from those bad feelings by avoiding social situations, but wind up paying a much higher emotional price of loneliness. If shyness has been a problem for you, and you expect to feel anxious making friends, I suggest you write out that coping self-statement on a small card and carry it with you. Give yourself a refresher dose regularly, but especially just before you go into a social situation or whenever you feel your social anxiety is getting too high.

'But I don't know what to say!'

All very well knowing what to say to myself to get started talking to people, I hear you grumble, but I don't know what to say to them. A fair question, and the answer is much simpler than you may think. In social conversations, people generally only discuss three topics. Get on top of these and you are ready for social discourse with anybody. First, talk about *trivia*, such as the weather, sport, current affairs, politics and so on. Some shy people make life more difficult for themselves by insisting that they don't want to be like everybody else and just talk about trivia. They want to get straight into deep and meaningful discussions, which will scare off most strangers. Don't underestimate the value of trivia as conversation starters. It's emotionally safe because it is personally trivial, even though it may be genuinely interesting (at least sometimes). It provides you with non-threatening conversation which may be all you want with this person, or into which you can bring the other two universal topics. You do not need to be an expert on trivia (unless you are keen on winning at parlour games). Read a newspaper or watch or listen to a news broadcast once a day, and you will be sufficiently familiar with what's going on to have a conversation.

Second, talk about your *common interests*, the work, recreations, hobbies, sports or mutual friends you have in common with this person. This is where open-ended questions come into their own, as the means of discovering your common interests. You will often see two people meet socially, introduce themselves, chat a little about trivia, and then discover a common interest, and they're off, set for at least an hour's worth of conversation as they swap ideas and information about their shared interest. If you want it to, such a discussion can open the way to an invitation to do that common interest together, and you have a date already.

Can't find any common interests, despite trying a few open-ended questions? It is quite possible that you will find you have little in common with some of the people you meet. You can certainly try to be friendly towards most of the people you meet, but don't expect to be friends with all of them. If this is the first time you have met this person, and you don't feel any particular need to make a success of this friendship, excuse yourself politely and move on, to start a conversation and explore the friendship possibilities with someone else. Meeting new friends takes persistence, more than anything else. It can be difficult, does involve some luck, and you will meet some people you don't like or with whom you have little in common. Give yourself a pat on the back for trying, and try again. On the other hand, if this person is very attractive or important to you but you are stymied by a lack of common interests, you can try to make some. Invite her to try some of your regular interests, or be willing to try some of hers, or use the search outlined above to discover some new ones that you both expect to enjoy.

Third, *talk about yourself*. I am not recommending that you brag and boast, which generally turns people off, but that you deliberately do some self-disclosure. This means telling the other person something personal about yourself, something that you obviously would not tell just anyone. If he wants to develop a friendship with you, he will respond to your self-disclosure with a similar piece of self-disclosure. This is how relationships develop intimacy. By sharing personal information you are effectively showing your friend that you trust her. Don't spill out your life story after two minutes of trivia. That will really scare off potential friends. You can imagine yourself as an onion, consisting of an outer skin you would let anyone see, covering a layer you would share with most people, and then another layer you would share with fewer people, and so on, until you reach a core you would share with only one or two very intimate friends, if anyone. Peel your onion slowly, and watch your friend's reaction. If your friend does not reciprocate your self-disclosure, or draws the line at a certain level of closeness, recognize that is as far as this relationship will develop, at least for now. Bearing in mind my discussion of Friendship Myth No. 5 above, don't throw the baby out with the bathwater by abandoning this relationship. Even casual friendships are a good recreational resource, and may develop further later. In the meantime, persistent application of the suggestions above should help you to find a circle of friends. They will be an important social and emotional

support for your single living, and later I will offer suggestions on
how to increase the intimacy in some of your friendships, possibly
leading to a successful erotic relationship.

Self-care skills

In addition to social skills, successful single living requires self-care
skills, particularly budgeting and money-management, house-
keeping, and tolerating and enjoying being alone. As far as the first
two areas, looking after your finances, your home, your clothes,
your meals and so on, are concerned, ask yourself two questions:
Do I need to know more about this? Or do I need to push myself
more?

If you answered yes to the first question, then you can build
your self-efficacy for these skills mostly by modelling: get information and tuition in the areas you need by buying some practical
handbooks or doing some adult education or just asking a friend for
a demonstration or advice. If you answered yes to the second question, you can build your self-efficacy here mostly by persuasion, by
talking yourself into doing what's necessary to look after yourself
properly. You might support that with some goal-setting, or even a
contract or two, as described in Chapter 7.

For example, a self-care skill often neglected by people living
alone is cooking. 'I can't be bothered preparing a meal just for
myself.' Yet good nutrition is essential for good health, plays a key
role in effective stress-management, and is a part of any realistic
definition of successful living. If you don't know the basics of good
nutrition, find out. If you don't know how to cook, learn (there is a
plethora of cooking books and courses). If you know what and how
to cook but can't be bothered, think again. Being realistically successful includes seeing yourself as important to you, and therefore
deserving quality self-care.

Loneliness versus solitude

Psychologists researching in this area have defined loneliness as
bad feelings that come from being alone. *Transient loneliness* is the
everyday, brief feeling that all of us have from time to time and is
not a problem. *Situational loneliness* is what may happen to someone who has previously had successful relationships which have
been lost as a result of changes in his living situation, such as
moving home, separation or divorce, or death of a spouse. It may

not be a problem, if the person is able to follow the same steps as he used previously to make relationships. If not, then he will need to follow the steps I am outlining in this chapter. *Chronic loneliness* is what may happen to someone who has had no successful relationships, at least for some years. She certainly needs to work carefully through this chapter.

However, being alone does not have to mean being lonely. *Solitude* is feeling good about being alone and it is a valuable stress-management factor, particularly for people with jobs that require them to deal with other people a lot. People generally use their solitude to relax and reflect, to consolidate their grip on current issues, or just fantasize. I mostly enjoy driving to and from my office, because it gives me half an hour of solitude each way. For half an hour each way I do not have to cope with anyone else's problems or demands, no one can walk in the door and I don't have to answer the phone. (Leave car phones for the Type As and other status-conscious people.)

How you feel about anything, including being alone, depends a lot on how you think about it. So when you are alone, watch your self-talk. If you are feeling very lonely for very long, you are probably thinking irrationally, like: 'I should be in good relationships all of the time and it is a disaster and great personal failure that I'm not in one right now.'

Instead think a more realistic, coping self-statement, like:

> 'It is disappointing if I'm alone when I don't want to be and I may feel lonely then, but I can cope with those feelings. I won't deny my loneliness; it's understandable if I don't want to be alone right now. But I won't exaggerate it, either, by dwelling on it. Some time by myself can be valuable, for relaxation and reflection. If I am alone more than I think is reasonable, then I should take some constructive steps to find some successful relationships.'

Then give yourself a shove in the back and take some constructive steps, like those in this chapter. However, recognize you cannot pursue new relationships in every spare moment and sometimes you may need to conclude your coping self-statement with:

> 'I am already doing as much as I can to find some successful relationships, I realize that will take some time to pay off,

and there is nothing I can do about it right now. OK, then right now I should find myself a distracting, pleasant activity to take my mind off being lonely.'

Then find an activity, constructive or enjoyable, that will hold your attention. Better still, have one or two available, like books to read or things to make or do, for those occasions when loneliness sneaks up on you.

Non-love relationships

These are not the relationships you have with people you haven't met yet, but are more likely to be your working relationships with many of the people in your day-to-day life, people with whom you share no significant intimacy, for whom you feel no passion, and towards whom you have no great commitment other than you might feel towards any fellow human. As 'non-love' relationships they fall outside the topic of this chapter, but not outside your life and hence they deserve some attention. Despite feeling no intimacy, passion or commitment towards someone, you may still feel respect for him and you still need to be able to conduct a successful relationship with him, however transient.

The basic skills for successful non-love relationships are set out in Chapters 4 and 5, especially assertion which, you will recall, is based on mutual respect, and co-operative problem-solving, which is a concrete expression of egalitarian relationships. Success in non-love relationships can enhance your self-efficacy for love relationships, because many activities are common to both kinds of relationships. Further, your non-love relationships are a rich potential source of new love relationships. Many good friends and lovers began as casual acquaintances. So your non-love relationships deserve a share of your effort to be successful in love.

Platonic and erotic love relationships

I will deal with these two kinds of love relationships together, because there is a considerable overlap in how you find and maintain each of them, although the absence of passion from platonic relationships is a crucial difference, too. If you are not interested in homosexual erotic relationships, it may be clear to you that your new friendship with someone of the same sex as you is never going to be erotic. Similarly, if you enjoy a successful marriage within which you and your partner expect sexual monogamy, it may be clear to you that your new friendship with someone of the opposite sex to you should never become erotic, although you may nonetheless have to deal with some passionate feelings at some stage. But often at the beginning of a relationship, we don't know whether it will turn out platonic or erotic. You may be looking for only a platonic relationship, and wind up with passionate feelings. Or you may be looking for an erotic relationship, already motivated by strong passion for your new friend, but have to settle for a platonic relationship, if he does not reciprocate your passion.

Platonic relationships are your friendships with other adults (or other teenagers, if you're a teenager, or other children, if you're a child). They consist of varying mixtures of intimacy and commitment, without passion, although that may develop later, as many an office romance will testify. A relationship that consists mostly of intimacy Professor Sternberg calls liking. You share some personal and private information with each other, generating some closeness and warmth, sometimes offering support, but without any major commitment to the relationship. As the level of intimacy increases, so usually does the level of commitment, and you are looking at the more special friendship, usually long-lasting and with mutual loyalty and support. This is also sometimes the state of a marriage where all passion has faded: 'We're great friends and companions, but there's no excitement any more.' A relationship that consists only of commitment is likely to be a totally empty marriage, now lacking both passion and intimacy, kept together only by obligation or fear of being alone. Sometimes commitment is all that is left in a parent-child relationship squashed by hostility or neglect.

In my discussion of successful single living, I have already outlined how to find new friendships. As I explained there, intimacy and commitment build slowly, through self-disclosure and sharing common interests. Now I will offer you some suggestions on how further to increase intimacy, for the sake of building a small number of very close relationships which are also likely to have high commitment. If it's your goal, one of them may also become an erotic relationship, possibly a successful long-term one.

Passion provides the initial motivation for developing erotic relationships, and should continue to provide some of the motivation for commitment, if it is looked after, as I will explain later. Intimacy should also provide increasing motivation for erotic relationships, and is initially the prime motivation for Platonic relationships. Remember, intimacy includes sharing, closeness, support, and feelings of warmth. So you build intimacy by sharing good times, and by good communication, involving mutual self-disclosure and acceptance. This will result in growing trust, the belief that you can count on your friend to do the right thing by you. The paradox about trust in relationships is that you have to act as though it is there — you have to make yourself vulnerable to the other person — so that she can demonstrate her trustworthiness, by then not letting you down. Then you have the evidence to support your trust.

It is important to understand this: developing any relationships necessarily involves taking the chance of being hurt, when you misplace your trust or when you would like a relationship to develop further than the other person does. There is *no* way of being certain beforehand, and if you hold yourself back from taking the chance of developing a relationship until you are 'certain' your feelings will be reciprocated, you will never get far in love. You can reduce the risk by developing intimacy at a realistically gradual pace, and demonstrate your growing commitment by giving the relationship reasonable priority, but even then you should *expect to try a number of casual relationships, and to cope with a few failures* in order to find a few special ones. Keep trying.

As well as building the intimacy of your self-disclosures gradually, you can similarly *build the intimacy of your shared activities*. You have probably begun by sharing structured activities — your common interests — in the company of other people. For some platonic relationships that is as intimate as you would want to get. For a more intimate relationship, you may choose to do some things as a couple, perhaps in the evening rather than daytime, and eventually less structured, like dinner together rather than tennis. But take your time, watching your friend's reaction to your initiatives, so as to develop the relationship at a mutually comfortable pace and to a mutually acceptable level of closeness.

Once again, *watch your self-talk*. At this stage of developing love relationships, you might fall into two more common thinking mistakes. The first is to think something like: 'If I get involved in a close relationship, I will lose all my freedom and independence.' You should recognise the exaggeration in this fear. All relationships involve some loss of freedom and independence, the loss increasing as your degree of mutual dependency increases. But no successful relationship, including marriage, requires the loss of *all* your freedom and independence. It is again a cost-benefit analysis: in a successful relationship you will feel the cost of some lost independence is adequately compensated by the rewards of the relationship.

The second is to think something like: 'Once this relationship becomes sexual, it will fail.' This fear may be based on your lack of sexual experience, or on your having had sexual difficulties or disappointments in the past. In the first case, you are making the common thinking mistake of *imagining the worst*, in the second case, you are making the common thinking mistake of *over-generalizing*. In either case, the answer is simple: *prepare for sexual relationships*.

Successful sex

I have defined erotic relationships as those including a major element of passion, of sexual attraction and physiological arousal. A relationship that consists only of passion is infatuation, a strong attraction to someone you really don't know (yet) and with whom you have not (yet) developed intimacy or commitment. Although the term 'infatuation' is sometimes applied by parents to express disapproval of their teenage children's relationships, this is mis-labelling on their part, because such relationships may well involve both intimacy and passion, a combination Professor Sternberg calls 'romantic love'. This is the shipboard romance or holiday love affair, with no real commitment to the future. Parents and participants ought to be more concerned about what Sternberg has called 'fatuous love', passion and commitment without any real intimacy, the rush to marriage on a wave of passion, sometimes shoved along by an unplanned pregnancy. 'Oh, well, we were going to get married, anyway.' And often disillusioned and divorced a few years later.

People's expectations of marriage, at least of its permanency, are clearly changing and I have no axe to grind there. Children are not necessarily harmed and sometimes benefit by their parents' divorce. But I think the trend is for kids to be more successful if they grow up with both a loving mum and dad together. Before you contemplate committing yourself to a relationship in which you are going to have babies, I strongly encourage you to ask yourself the second hour question: 'What do we do for the second hour?' If your relationship so far consists of only infatuation or fatuous love, the first hour is easy: enjoy your passion for each other. But you won't have much of an idea of what to do in the second hour, and that's a potentially serious problem for a long-term relationship, especially as passion drops back. Take your time to find out whether you can also develop intimacy, through good communication and common interests, before you decide to express a longer term commitment like planning babies.

As I explained earlier, passion does diminish, in all relationships, probably as novelty fades. For letting go of an infatuation or a holiday romance or fatuous love, dwindling passion may be helpful. For a long-term, erotic love relationship, it can be a serious problem. In a Macquarie University study of divorcing Australian couples, sexual dissatisfaction was the most commonly cited reason for the marriage failing (although other problems were also included by any one couple). What your sexual relationship loses in novelty, it can more than make up through increasing comfort with each other, and a willingness to explore, extend and refresh your sexuality. Even if your expectations are shorter-term, you can reasonably aim for successful sex.

The problem is that almost none of us had a formal sexual education. If you had a formal sex education at all, it was about how to make babies, which was one of the first big lies most of us heard about sex, that it was for making babies. When was the last time you had sex to make a baby? Right. And if you ask most people you will get the same answer. Most of us choose to make babies only a few times in our lives, if at all. But most of us choose to have sex rather more often and frequently we are being careful to avoid making babies. So most of us are having sex most of the time not to make babies, but to make good feelings, for ourselves and our lovers, to keep alive the passionate component of a long-term relationship, such as a marriage.

We all did have a sex education, even if you didn't notice it at the time. Often from parents we learned embarrassment or guilt and little else; from peers we learned misinformation and jokes (although, in the absence of any factual information, how do you tell which part of a joke may not be true?) And then most of us did our 'practical' course, petting as teenagers. The end result of this more or less uniform and universal sex education is a universal set of beliefs about sex that most of us swallowed. The trouble is, they're wrong, however popular they may be. Approaching your sexual relationships unrealistically is no recipe for success, so I will now describe these popular beliefs and explain why each is untrue. In reading this list, don't smugly tell yourself that you're not silly enough to believe any of them. Ask yourself, instead, how much such ideas influence your sexual behaviour, even if you see they are silly when you read them.

The collected sexual mythology

Myth No. 1 Intercourse is the adult, the best, the most important part of sex.

An over-emphasis on intercourse reflects both a continuing confusion between reproduction (which generally does require intercourse) and sexuality (which does not), and an unnecessary reliance on male initiative, since most men find intercourse very arousing. But most women do not, and there's no logical reason why they should. Accepting this myth makes men worry about getting and keeping their erections, and women worry about not being aroused and satisfied by intercourse. Less than three women in ten find intercourse sufficiently physically arousing to have orgasm, and I suspect many of them are increasing their arousal by also stimulating the clitoris or having a good fantasy.

Myth No. 2 Men take the initiative

Or at least we learned to expect them to during our practical course, petting as teenagers. Accepting this myth makes men worry about what to do, how to do it, and when, and it makes women worry about being disappointed by his choice.

Myth No. 3 He is responsible for her satisfaction as well as his own.

Learned at the same time as Myth No. 2, both resting on the assumption that he knows what she will like. Well, only if she tells him. The only person who can usefully take responsibility for your sexual satisfaction is you: you need to know what you like, and be assertive enough to ask for it. A good lover — there are no 'expert' lovers — is one who will listen to and be guided by your requests.

Myth No. 4 Women are less interested in sex than men are. They are slower in sexual arousal and need more stimulation.

Or so it said in your handy marriage manual: 'Foreplay is for the benefit of the woman.' Unlike him, she needs to be warmed up. In fact, your level of sexual interest is determined mostly by how well sex works for you, by your sexual success rate. Sexually successful women — women who understand, enjoy and assert their own sexuality — are no less interested in sex nor any slower in arousal than are sexually successful men. The partner who plays a more passive role, relying on the other person's choice of technique, will usually be slower in arousal.

Myth No. 5   His penis is the best, the appropriate part of his body to use to stimulate her.

We are certainly not the only culture to make a fuss about penises, but that doesn't make this any less of a myth. Penises are great for *receiving* stimulation, as most men discover early in life. But they are poorly designed and positioned for *giving* effective stimulation, as most men gradually realize. Accepting this myth makes men worry about the size, shape and erectile capacity of their penises, instead of recognizing that other parts of their bodies are better designed for giving effective sexual stimulation.

Myth No. 6   Her vagina is the best, the appropriate part of her body for receiving sexual stimulation.

You will recognize that it is this myth combined with the one before that set you up for Myth No. 1 and the sadly frequent over-emphasis on intercourse. In fact, most of the vagina is fairly insensitive, as you would know if you are a woman who uses tampons. When women set out to stimulate themselves, to masturbate, they mostly choose to stimulate the clitoris, rarely to penetrate the vagina — they know what they like. Accepting this myth makes women worry about the size and shape and unresponsiveness of their vaginas and makes men worry about their sexual performance.

Myth No. 7   All good sex ends in orgasm. In really good sex, both partners will orgasm at the same time.

An over-emphasis on orgasm, was only one of the unfortunate by-products of the pop psychology of sex. Orgasms do feel great and are even healthy for you, but 'musturbation' in sex is definitely bad for you. Telling yourself you 'must' have an orgasm (or get an erection or lubricate your vagina or whatever) is the best way of stopping that from happening. Trying to coincide two involuntary responses like your respective orgasms is a good way of squashing your sexual fun.

Myth No. 8   Sex ends at 50 (or menopause or some other life point).

If sex has never been very successful for you, you may be relieved to find an excuse to give it up. For sexually successful people, there is no reason for stopping sex as you get older. You may slow down, but slowing down is not the same as stopping.

In place of these myths I like to propose a more realistic view of sexual success:

> 'A good sexual relationship is one in which both partners have orgasms on most sexual occasions, somehow or other. It does not matter what sexual techniques they use, so long as these are comfortable and acceptable to both partners. And it does not matter which partner does not have an orgasm on any occasion, so long as they are both satisfied that they each have orgasm as often as they want.'

For a practical programme to share with your partner, for either building a good sexual relationship or refreshing a jaded one, I recommend sensate focus, a series of mutual pleasuring exercises, described in Chapter 4 of my book with Lynette Evans, *Living & Loving Together* (published by Nelson). Be wary about self-help for sexual problems. Most of the pop psychology books on this topic have been found not only to be no help but actually to make the problems worse. If you want to try self-help first, make a judicious selection of a manual written by qualified people and stick to it closely. Otherwise, consider getting some professional help. Nowadays most sexual problems can be solved fairly easily, if you get the right advice.

Successful marriage

A successful, long-term, erotic love relationship is likely (although not necessarily) to be a marriage. I wish I could say the reverse is also likely, but sadly it isn't. Sometimes when I suggest to a couple that their marriage is seriously vulnerable, they look surprised and say, 'But our marriage is as good as our friends'.' They're probably right, but what they don't realize is that their friends' relationships are probably vulnerable, too. The standard of marriage in our soci-

MYTHS ABOUT MARRIAGE
(OR LIVING TOGETHER)

1
If you feel you only *like* your partner now, that means you have fallen out of love.

2
If you and your partner love each other, you will spend all of your time together.

3
If you and your partner love each other, you will automatically know how each other thinks and feels.

4
If you and your partner love each other, you will automatically communicate well.

5
If a relationship is in trouble, usually *one* of the partners is to blame (usually the *other* one!).

6
If you and your partner love each other, good sex comes naturally.

7
Arguments clear the air, and enable you to make up and feel good.

8
An argument can only end by one partner giving in and admitting that she/he is wrong.

9
If your partner feels love for someone else, she/he must feel less love for you.

10
If your partner feels sexually attracted to someone else, she/he must feel less attracted to you.

11
If you want your partner to do something, nagging is the best way to get him/her to do it. If you want your partner to stop nagging, give in to it!

---

ety is nothing to blow trumpets about and being as good as the rest is no great success. To repeat, my definition of personal success is not a recipe for complacency: if you look at any area of your life, including your marriage, and have to conclude that it could quite reasonably be running a lot better, you should pull up your socks and get to work on improving it.

In the table I have listed the popular myths of marriage. Like the other myths I have discussed, these are beliefs that set you up for failure. Again, in reading them, ask yourself the useful question: 'How much do I allow my marriage to be influenced by these myths, even if I can see they are unrealistic when I read them?'

Professor Sternberg calls consummate or complete love the relationship in which all three components, passion, intimacy and commitment, are strong and in balance. He acknowledges that this is an ideal to work towards, rather than some perfect end state to achieve and then forget about, although he seems to me to be unnecessarily pessimistic about many couples enjoying complete love. Providing you see it as a relationship in which both partners are forever taking practical steps to maintain those three components of love, I don't see such working success as rare at all. Sometimes you and your spouse will be more successful than at other times, but as long as the consistent effort is there, you will be achieving your realistic, personal best for that marriage. Looking after your sexual relationship will maintain the passion; good communication, eliminating arguments, sharing decisions and common interests, especially as a couple, will maintain intimacy; and the rewards of passion and intimacy, coupled with realistic thinking about your relationship, should facilitate commitment. But success and your children (if you have some) is so important that I want to take that up in the next chapter.

9| SUCCESSFUL PARENTING

There are two possible notions of success in parenting, obviously related but not as tightly linked as you may think. First, you may try to do your personal, realistic best at being a parent, and I will offer you many suggestions in this chapter on how to do that. Second, you may also regard it as a personal success if your children are successful, but here I urge caution, in both directions. If your children are stunning successes, accept some reflected credit but don't hog it. If your children are stunning flops, accept some of the responsibility, but not all of it. The truth is, you are only one of many influences on your children, from their conception on, and your influence tends to wane as they grow. Given that you probably would like eventually to see them as successfully independent, the dwindling of your influence is desirable and inevitable. I have emphasized the desirability of setting realistic goals to build your success rate and your motivation, and that is just as important to parenting. Aim to do your personal, realistic best and you will be as successful at parenting as you can; with some luck, that will show itself in your children also being reasonably successful, but that is not under your direct control and should not be the final measure of your success.

In fact, many of the problems of parenting arise from unrealistic goal-setting. Although most of us eventually become parents, few of us were taught how to parent successfully. Parents today live in far greater social isolation than before. Families have shrunk to consist often of only two adults, or increasingly one, with their or her (less often his) children. So there are fewer adults at home to share the parenting, and less access to the last generation of parents for practical advice. People move house more often nowadays, so family and friends may become geographically distant and unable to offer much support. Even those of us who develop good relationships with our neighbours may be reluctant to admit we are having difficulty or uncertainty in parenting, especially the fathers.

To increase the difficulty of setting realistic parenting goals, much of the world is changing and that change is accelerating. The next few decades will see social, political, economic, industrial and environmental changes on a scale and at a rate never seen before. The tradition of parents handing down to their children the wisdom gained from their own experience may often no longer work. Mum and Dad grew up in a world that was genuinely different in some important ways, and the skills or ideas that worked for them as kids may no longer meet the needs of their children. However, you can exaggerate this parental obsolescence. It will be most apparent in the 'technological' areas of life — schoolwork, job-related skills, recreations that are heavily dependent on equipment, especially electronics. Technological obsolescence of your ideas may make you feel inadequate, watching your child play with a microcomputer, and in some areas of life you may have to say honestly, 'I don't know.'

But don't make the mistake of thinking that obsolescence applies to everything you have to offer. Humans are humans, and they are not showing much fundamental change at all. Your contribution to your children's human development will remain vital and timely. Indeed, it is their technological learning that will date quickly: most of what your child learns at school will be superseded by the time he joins the workforce. More than anything else, what your child will need to be successful in a rapidly changing world will be good self-efficacy and good interpersonal skills, exactly the ingredients I have proposed for your personal success. The technological and even some social aspects of the world may change quickly, but the essence of being a successful person will not. You may not be able to help your child programme her microcomputer, but you can help her to develop a good and robust appreciation of herself and the skills to live and work successfully with others, and those achievements will be helping her to be successful long after microcomputers have gone to the museum.

As I pointed out in the previous chapter, you did get a sex education, whether you noticed or not. Likewise, you did get a parenting education, whether you noticed or not. You grew up with the example of your own parents, and that is powerful modelling, even when you think you are never going to be like them. And you saw some modelling by other kids' parents, and perhaps by grandparents or uncles or aunts. Popular fiction and film also present lots of examples. Television parents, I find, are often presented misleadingly. Although there has been a welcome attempt recently to involve psychologists as script consultants in some of the American production houses, especially for family programmes, that is recent and not yet widespread. The end result of this is another set of myths, this time of parenthood. Again these are popular beliefs, widely held, but unrealistic. A great deal of parent-child and especially parent-adolescent conflict arises from parents swallowing these myths and approaching their parenting unrealistically. The myths of parenthood are discussed below and I suggest you read it now, again asking yourself not, 'Do I believe these myths?' but 'How much do I let these myths influence my parenting? Even if I can see they are myths when I read them, do I act as though they are true?'

The Myths of Parenthood

Myth No. 1   If I make a mistake, it will always affect my child.

The belief that childhood was a crucially important developmental stage, during which you are forming a 'personality' that will stick with you for the rest of your life, stems largely from Freud who got that wrong, along with most other things. He never had any scientific evidence to support this belief (or any of his other, even sillier ideas) and when it was scientifically tested it was proved wrong. We do not collect an unchangeable 'personality' in childhood. In fact, people can and do change significantly throughout their lives. Learning in childhood is influential on later behaviour; so is later learning.

Normal parents make some mistakes and normal children are robust enough to survive them. A consistently repeated mistake can give your child a lasting problem, so it's worth your while to learn about successful parenting and make a reasonable effort to do it. But even lasting problems can be resolved later, maybe with some assistance.

Myth No. 2 As a parent, I have the power to make my kids do whatever I want (and the responsibility to make them do what's right).

Good luck, you are going to need it. In fact, there are no reliable ways of controlling human behaviour and, with any luck, we'll never find any. You can get the *illusion* of controlling your child's behaviour by threatening her with physical violence ('Do as I say or I will hit you!'), or emotional violence ('Do as I say or I won't love you!'), or material violence ('Do as I say or I'll take away your favourite toy!') If you use threats like these in an attempt to get control of your child's behaviour, you will sometimes get apparent control, in that your child will do what you say, while you're around. Behind your back he will do what he likes and, if he didn't like being threatened by you, he may go out of his way to do the opposite of your wishes. That is the usual outcome of authoritarian, punitive approaches to discipline: an appearance of compliance masking largely undisciplined behaviour. If you have any doubts about this, look at the general level of compliance by adults with laws relating to the speed limit. All you ever have over your children is influence, not control, and heavy-handed attempts at enforcing control will just lessen your influence.

Myth No. 3 My children cause my unhappiness, so they must change for me to feel better.

Throughout this book I have emphasized that you are responsible for how you feel. Other people, including your children, can *influence* how you feel, but they cannot *control* it. You also influence how you feel about your children's actions, by how you think and act in response to them, and that is under *your* control. If your child does some things that influence you to feel bad, think about it realistically and make a constructive effort to get him to change his behaviour, by following the suggestions in this chapter.

Myth No. 4   Children are naturally undisciplined and behave like wild animals. Parents must beat them into shape to make them civilized.

Children do not 'naturally' do anything except maybe cry, suckle and make a mess in nappies. Humans do not genetically inherit detailed behaviour patterns the way some other animals do. We may inherit some broad behavioural dispositions, but the over-whelming majority of our behaviour is learned. If your child has learned to behave in some unacceptable ways, that's a pity and may be distressing for both of you. But it's never too late for him to learn to behave differently, by following the suggestions in this chapter, none of which involve 'beating into shape' (see Myth No. 2 again).

Myth No. 5   It is my responsibility to solve my children's problems and to protect them from life's threats.

It is a natural temptation to want to save your child from being hurt, and in genuinely serious situations the obvious thing to try. But often when parents rescue their children the real motivation is selfish: 'It distresses me to see you, my child, unhappy. So to lessen my distress I will rescue you from your unhappiness.' In the process I will cheat you of the opportunity to learn two vital lessons: first, that when you do something wrong, there is usually a bad consequence; and second, that even when you do make a mistake, you can cope with that.

I have seen 'clinically' a steady trickle of people who were over- protected as children in just that way, never learning that there can be real world consequences of silly or wrong behaviour, and never having the chance to develop a robust self-esteem so that you can take a knock and get over and on with it. Within common-sense limits, let your children benefit from the real world consequences of their behaviour even when those consequences are unpleasant, and you are helping them to develop a realistic appreciation of the world, which can only foster their personal success. Be available as a source of support, advice and assistance when that's requested, but don't intrude uninvited for essentially selfish reasons.

In place of these myths I want to propose four basic rules of thumb, four practical tips for parenting success: be consistent, give unconditional love, use good interpersonal skills yourself, use trial-and-success learning.

No. 1 tip for successful parenting   Be consistent

Try to be consistent in your dealings with your children. Give yourself permission to have the normal variability in your moods and behaviour, but recognize that it's easier for your children to learn what is expected of them if those expectations are reasonably consistent. Researchers have found that parental inconsistency causes more difficulty for children than parents who are too lenient or too harsh but at least consistently so. If you accept or even laugh at a particular behaviour today but punish the same behaviour tomorrow, you are making it hard for your kid to know what is or isn't acceptable behaviour.

The same applies to consistency between both parents. If a behaviour is accepted or even encouraged by Dad but punished by Mum, your child is receiving very mixed messages and will be confused. Again, accept the typical differences of opinion that can occur in any successful relationship; discussing and explaining those differences with your child may be a good model for him. But if there are major differences between you and your spouse about what is expected of and how to deal with your children, the onus is on the two of you to sort out those differences reasonably and sensibly. Some reading, like this chapter or *Living and Loving Together*, and some discussion to reach reasonable agreement may be all you need. If not, then consider getting some qualified, professional help. I frequently find the distress in a child who is brought to me reflects the distress in her parents' relationship, and the solution to the former lies in resolving the latter.

No. 2 tip for successful parenting   Give unconditional love

Unconditional love is the kind of love which effectively says, 'I love you (the person in front of me). Sometimes I may dislike or disapprove of some of your behaviour, and that may temporarily lead to some bad feelings between us, but it does not lessen my love for you.' This does not mean that you should feel love for your children all of the time. We all sometimes get bored or angry with each other, or are busy on other parts of our balanced lives. It does mean that you draw a clear distinction between your feelings for your child and your feelings for his behaviour.

Conditional love is the kind of love which effectively says, 'I will only love you if you behave as I want. When I don't like your behaviour that means I have stopped loving you.' If you offer your children conditional love, you are teaching them that their personal value depends on other people's judgements of their behaviour and you are laying down the foundations of a shaky self-image and building over-concern for other people's approval. Children who grow up with conditional love have great difficulty with self-love and therefore in their love relationships with others, as children and later as adults. Children who learn their value depends on the judgements of others are ready to swallow the success = winning = beating others myth and are well on the way to developing their Type A Behaviour Pattern, not what I would regard as the fruits of successful parenting.

Adult-child love relationships

The most important of these are, of course, parent-child relationships, the focus of this chapter, but they may also include uncles and aunts relating to nephews and nieces, or grandparents and grandchildren, or relationships with the children of neighbours or friends. With the growing number of step-families, there is a parallel growth in step-parent relationships, with their own extra obstacles to success. In principle, all the suggestions in this chapter apply equally well to step-families. However, it can be a mistake not to recognize or to try to ignore the differences in being a stepfamily. My suggestions should be combined with a realistic acceptance of those differences.

There are other adults who might legitimately and beneficially have love relationships, of the kind I will outline, with children in their care, either as part of their work, such as teachers, nurses, child care workers and so on, or as part of their recreation, such as sports coaches or youth club leaders. In a sense these adults are often acting as temporary surrogate parents, and much of this chapter can be applied to those relationships as well.

It may seem obvious but I feel it is necessary to point out that the love component that should be absent from adult-child relationships is passion, particularly the sexual part of it. I have already pointed out that adult-child relationships are asymmetrical in several ways: children are often encouraged to be more emotionally intimate with their parents than their parents may be willing to reciprocate and are generally more dependent on parental support than the reverse. Parents are generally more committed to their relationships with their children and stay that way longer, than vice versa.

There is also asymmetry where passion may enter an adult-child love relationship. Adults are older and more experienced than children. It is therefore not unreasonable to expect them to be wiser and more responsible. Adults can accept that they may have feelings of sexual attraction to children, particularly physically maturing adolescents, and yet responsibly and wisely decide not to act on those feelings. I have occasionally given some worried fathers counselling along these lines, to their relief: having the feelings is OK, it just means you are lucky enough to have (or know or work with) some attractive kids. But as a responsible adult and as a concrete expression of your love for those children, you do not act out the passionate component of your love.

The intimacy component of adult-child relationships will vary from just a supportive liking, without a great deal of closeness or sharing, as might occur between a teacher and a pupil, to the far more emotional intimacy of a successful parent-child relationship. The teacher and pupil may say they like each other; the parent and child will say they love each other, preferably often and clearly. In any case, you will use two basic mechanisms to build and maintain the intimacy component of your love relationships with children, good communication and shared recreation.

No. 3 tip for successful parenting   Use good interpersonal skills yourself

To carry out the suggestions in this chapter with your children, you will need to communicate your feelings, good and bad, clearly and constructively; you will need to assert yourself reasonably and responsibly; you will need to be able to make and refuse requests, and to be willing and able to negotiate about each other's requests.

These interpersonal skills are the basis of successful parenting and further, by using them consistently yourself, you are modelling them for your child. Your example will always carry much more clout than your words.

The communication skills, spelled out in Chapter 4, backed up when necessary by conflict resolution and co-operative problem-solving, from Chapter 5, are the means for sharing feelings and intimate thoughts, for developing closeness and providing practical support. Especially level about your love or liking: people, including children, tend to love or like those who love or like them. There is no better way of showing that than simply saying so. Children who grow up being told they are loved and liked by the significant adults in their lives are likely to be successful at seeing themselves as lovable and likeable. The last two skills, conflict resolution and co-operative problem-solving, become increasingly important as your children grow and develop their independence, especially in adolescence, since they are concrete demonstrations of your respect for your children. Similarly, your approach to discipline should be based on assertive principles, not aggressively authoritarian ones. Giving orders, usually backed by implicit or explicit threats, you will recognize as one of the *anti-communication* behaviours described in Chapter 4, a good way of losing influence with your children. Giving orders to your children is an expression of Parenting Myth No. 2, and you may like to review my discussion of that myth. Level about your opinions and values, and be willing to listen to your children's; make requests and be willing to negotiate reasonably about them, especially as your kids grow, and you will have maximum influence with your children. You never had control, anyway.

Sharing recreation is the other means of building mutual liking. People, including children, like to be with people they have fun with. If you are mostly a source of practical and material support, your children may feel appreciative or grateful, but not loving. If you are mostly a source of discipline, however fair and assertive, your children may respect you but still not like you much. If you want them to enjoy your relationship, do enjoyable things together, reasonably often. It is important that 'enjoyable' means enjoyable for you both, not one of you suffering the other's choice. A good relationship encourages activities independent of each other, when you can pursue your individual interests. Building the liking side of intimacy requires both of you sharing the enjoyment of the activity. This can take some imaginative searching, and usually requires occasional revision to cope with changing interests, but it's worth it.

I remember being delighted to find that my son, Erin, then a toddler, could grasp the basics of Snakes and Ladders well enough for us to share an enjoyable game or two, without either of us becoming bored. He has been skiing with us several times now, enjoys catching fish with me (so long as they're biting), and now has started snorkeling. I'm not really into Lego and he thinks my taste in television is boring, so these are activities we tend to do independently of each other. But fun times with him are an important goal for me, and a crucial part of my balanced lifestyle.

The commitment component of your love relationships with children will develop as it does with adults. There is your initial choice, to have children (and that should be a considered choice, not something you slip into), or to become involved with an adult who has children (as in step-families), or to work or play with children. More than anything else, the deliberate nature of this choice should be reflected in your goal-setting, back in Chapter 7, and in your formula for a successfully balanced lifestyle, back in Chapter 3. You must make and protect time for your relationships with your children. In a pre-Christmas survey which asked children what they would really like most of all, more time with their parents topped the poll. The kids knew they could not be bought off with material gifts or benefits, and so should you. A bit less time spent at work might mean a bit less in the Christmas stocking, but it could also mean more time and much more successful love relationships with your children. Well, the kids have told you which they would prefer to have. Time with you does not all have to be in big slabs; you can respond positively to your child's approaches even when they are not convenient, and keep that contact brief. Locked away down here in the dungeon (actually my study), chained to the word-processor by fear of my editor's wrath for running late again, I may be interrupted by Erin wanting to show me his latest Lego construction. The five minutes I spend admiring his handiwork may mean a little less writing today, but it's an investment I happily make in my relationship with my son. For his part, he seems to have no difficulty accepting my explanation that I am working and can only afford five minutes now.

Maintaining commitment means you will need consciously to choose the options that protect and promote those love relationships. Protecting time for them; choosing to communicate effectively rather than blow your stack, withdraw in a huff, or lay down the law; revising your expectations to keep them realistically age-appropriate as your children grow. I will return to the last point below, but for now let me conclude that your love relationships with children also deserve a share of your effort. I have been dismayed and saddened by the number of adults I have seen who began their love relationships with their children with such high hopes, only to be disappointed and ultimately hurt. Your children certainly have increasing influence over your relationship with them, but you do get a head start. Use it! I have often pointed out that I have never met anyone who got married because he wanted to be divorced. I have also never met anyone who became a parent (or otherwise involved with children) because she wanted eventually to be rejected and hurt. We generally muck up our love relationships because we don't know how to make them work. You are already in the process of learning how to make them work; then it's up to you to try it.

No. 4 tip for successful parenting   Use trial-and-success learning

You will recognize this as Tip No. 1 for building your own motivation back in Chapter 6. Having successful accomplishments builds your self-efficacy and that in turn builds your motivation, and that applies to your kids as much as to you. So, helping your child to have successes is a very important way you can help him to become successful in his own right, and there are several ways you can help.

Try to have realistic expectations of your children. It is unrealistic to expect anyone to do anything perfectly at the first attempt. It is realistic to expect your child to try reasonably well providing she is systematically being encouraged to try, a point I will return to shortly. This may or may not be successful the first time, or the second time, or the nth time. Your encouragement and patience will support her attempts and improvement. Try to make your expectations realistic for your child's age. Humans do a lot of growing and maturing long after birth, unlike most other animals. In particular, children do not and cannot think like adults. Expecting a five-year-old to think like you is as unrealistic as expecting him to be as tall as you.

If you want your child to be motivated enough to achieve her personal, realistic best, then reward her trying, not the actual performance. It's reasonable for you and she to agree on some possible goals for a final level of performance, but usually you won't know how realistic those goals are before she attempts them. Sticking to arbitrary goals may cause you both unrealistically to devalue her genuine efforts and simply discourage her from trying further; or you may unnecessarily limit a child who was capable of doing much better. Reward your child for trying, be willing to adjust your expectations realistically up or down, and she will discover her own limits.

Nowhere is this clearer than in regard to schoolwork. I see a steady trickle of parents with adolescent child in tow, complaining that he is 'under-performing' and as this is his final year something must be done urgently to stop this under-performance. My first step is to ask the parents how they *know* their child is under-performing. They will invariably reply, 'His teachers say so,' and they may then produce a collection of school reports that are dotted with teachers' comments like: 'Could improve' or 'Should do better'. I then ask, 'How do the teachers know your child is in fact capable of doing better?' The parents look puzzled by this and eventually have to concede that the teachers are relying on their personal impressions and hunches about this child. No one has actually measured the child's ability.

When I do just that, test the child on a standard intelligence test, he usually turns out to be around average, not dull, not a genius, just a kid of good average ability who can perform at a good average level. In fact, if you look closely at his school reports, that's often what he has done: obtained good average grades. But no one has said: 'Good for you, Charlie! You did your personal, realistic best. That was a successful year for you.' So he has been cheated of experiencing realistic success, his self-efficacy for schoolwork has been knocked down and his motivation will be fading. Indeed, by the time some of these children are dragged into my office they have lost a lot of motivation and are now actually under-performing as a result. But notice that the major cause of their under-performance was the inability of their parents and teachers to adopt realistic expectations and to reward effort rather than some arbitrary performance. With impeccable intentions the parents and teachers have set out to encourage the child to do his best, a perfectly reasonable goal. But their method, insisting that the child should do better when he may already be doing his realistic best, is ill-founded and damaging.

A child's school grades reflect the following factors:
genetic inheritance,
'choice' of parents,
home atmosphere,
'choice' of school,

'choice' of teacher(s),
'choice' of teaching methods,
'choice' of assessment method,
health and wellbeing at the time of learning and assessment,
and effort.

Yet parents and teachers persistently ignore the influence of the first eight of these factors and interpret a child's performance as reflecting only the last. I repeat, if you want your child to do as well as she is capable, then reward her effort, not her performance. In the same vein, let me repeat my caution in Chapter 1 about the damaging effects of comparing one child's performance with another's. Whether that comparison is made by a well-intended teacher or parent — 'Andrew can do it, why can't you?' — it is ill-founded and potentially damaging. Unless the two children being compared are matched equally on all of the relevant factors, like those listed above, the comparison of performances is invalid and misleading. The child who seems to have done better may simply have fluked better genes or luckier breaks at home or school. He is learning that he doesn't need to bother trying hard, while the other child is learning she doesn't do well enough, even if she has done her personal best. I am pleased to report that schools do seem to be moving away from the fallacious and harmful practice of routinely and publicly comparing children's performances, although I have been disappointed by how many parents and teachers don't understand why this is being done and still want to cling to the old, hurtful ways. I am not unrealistic enough to imagine that kids won't compare themselves with each other; of course they will, and that can help them to develop a realistic appreciation of themselves. What we adults can do is show what's important by what we attend to and praise, and that's effort.

Help your child to find avenues for success. Some of us are suited to academic work, some of us aren't. Some of us are suited to the sports or other extra-curricular activities offered at school or by the various children's clubs and organizations; some of us aren't. None of these activities is a prerequisite for being successful in life. Good self-efficacy is. So encourage your child to shop around amongst the activities open to her, to find the ones she can succeed at. Beware of insisting that she sticks at some activity that she is not getting success from, just because you used to do it or children in your family have always done it or it's supposed to be good for children or some similar reason. It's her childhood, for her enjoyment and benefit; not for you to relive or compensate for your own childhood.

Tell your child when you think he has been successful. Don't assume he will know how you feel; little humans don't read minds any better than do adult humans (see Chapter 4). Don't assume he should do 'the right thing' just because it's right and not need any praise. That level of self-direction in his behaviour is one of your long-term goals for successful parenting, but most of us have not completely mastered it even by adulthood. Rewards and praise that come too easily don't mean much; your approval currency is inflated. So do reward judiciously. But no rewards or praise amount to ignoring your child's successful behaviour, and that very effectively punishes it. Probably the most powerful reward parents have to offer their children is their attention. If the only way your child can get much of your attention is to behave badly, don't be surprised if he behaves badly. If you would like to see more successful behaviour, attend to it when it occurs. Children who grow up with praise do not develop swelled heads; they become confident adults.

Starting success young

You can really begin laying the foundations for your child's success before her birth, by making sure that her conception was intended and wanted by both of you and by looking after Mum's health and well-being during the pregnancy. But now I want to offer you some suggestions for laying the foundations for success in the pre-school years, particularly the first three years of life. Yes, children do learn, potentially a lot, in their first three years and that learning can give them a head start at being successful. Conversely it has been observed that some children are already educationally disadvantaged by the time they begin kindergarten. You will effectively be your child's first teacher, whether you like it or not, so you might as well try to do it successfully.

I am not proposing a pressure-cooker approach to infancy, cramming alphabet blocks into your child's head so that he can get honours in his kindergarten entry exam. In fact, the research in this field casts serious doubt on the usefulness of so-called educational toys, including those elaborate 'flash-card' vocabulary sets and similar devices claimed to prepare children for school skills. If you have already bought some, or the doting grandparents turn up with one, don't despair. 'Educational' toys are not harmful, just not educational. Let your kids enjoy playing with them, if they want to, but do not fall into the trap of thinking that 'educational' toys can do your educational job for you (while you do something else). Don't be alarmed by the prospect of this job I'm lining up for you. As you will see, successful pre-school parenting requires no elaborate equipment or skills and does not have to take an unreasonable amount of your time.

Recognition of the influential role being played by the early years of life prompted psychologists at Harvard University to set up the Pre-school Project, to find out what parental behaviours were making their children advantaged or disadvantaged. They studied a large sample of pre-school children, from a wide range of socio-economic and cultural backgrounds, and found a consistent pattern of parenting associated with children who were superior in linguistic and intellectual abilities and in social skills. I like the fact that they identified as the key a comfortable, constructive style of parenting that made the early educational process enjoyable as well as effective, rather than an intensive, highly structured 'superbaby' programme.

From this research they developed a training programme for parents, which could be conducted in the community at a relatively low cost, and this programme was then evaluated over several years in Missouri. Independent evaluators found that the social development of the project children was 'outstanding' and their linguistic and intellectual development was significantly superior to that of children not in the project. They emphasised that families taking part in the project came from all sections of the community, so the results offered very strong support for the effectiveness of this style of parenting. They caution that the programme cannot eliminate other problems, like a distressed marriage or an alcoholic parent or abject poverty, but it is certainly suitable for the majority of families. Here are their guidelines.

Do provide your child with the maximum opportunity to explore her environment, by making your home as safe and accessible as possible. Move fragile or dangerous items up and out of reach, replacing them with things your child can handle. For example, detergents and cleaners belong in a high cupboard; put plastic containers or old pots and pans under the sink.

Be available to your child as much as you reasonably can. Don't hover or smother, but be nearby to provide attention or support when he needs it. Respond to his approaches promptly and positively, as often and as much as you can, even if you then have to explain you are temporarily unavailable because you are doing something. Be enthusiastic and encouraging.

Do set limits and stick to them consistently. This can begin as early as eight months and should certainly apply during the period of 'negativism', usually between 15 and 24 months, when children are often just trying to find out what they can get away with. Some parents are reluctant to crack down on unacceptable behaviour, fearing they might lose their child's love, so instead train a monster whom no one likes. Do not give in to unreasonable requests nor tolerate unacceptable behaviour; level promptly and clearly to let her know what you don't like, and make a clear request for what you want her to do instead. If your request is not accepted, or at least discussed with you reasonably, back it up with Time Out (described below).

Do talk to your child often. Because we tend not to talk to things that don't talk back and most children don't talk until they are one or two or older, many parents think it's a waste of time talking to them before that. In fact, children begin to understand simple words and phrases long before their first birthday, usually between six and eight months, even if they cannot reply. Start talking to him early, and gradually increase your conversation by adding new words through related ideas. For example, your child is wearing a blue plastic box on his head, so you say: 'Your hat is blue, like your shorts. My shorts are green, like the table.'

Do provide new learning opportunities by involving your child in some of your activities, like shopping, or cooking, or fixing or making something. She will gain far more from this kind of learning experience than from a structured exercise with an elaborate 'educational' toy. Do allow your child to choose and direct some of your shared activities. Do encourage your child's pretend and fantasy play, especially when she acts out adult roles.

Do not confine your child regularly for long periods in a play pen or a room. Even filling the playpen or room with 'educational' toys will not compensate for the restriction on his learning experience. Similarly don't encourage your child to focus most of his activity on you to the exclusion of independent activity.

Do not ignore your child's attempts to get your attention until she has to throw a tantrum or misbehave to get through to you. Again, you can always attend briefly and explain you are temporarily unavailable. Don't assume she knows you are unavailable because you are doing something; after all, you do interrupt some of her activities, don't you?

Do not worry that your child won't love you if you say 'No' *sometimes.* Children begin with a very self-centred view of the universe, that it's there to serve their every whim and fancy. You do your child no favour if you protect that illusion by spoiling him.

Do not insist on winning every argument just to prove who's boss. I hope your self-esteem isn't that shaky. Be willing to discuss and reason, to validate your child's point of view, and to give in when that's appropriate.

Do not insist that your child should never make a mess. Clutter is usually a sign of a healthy and curious baby. You can develop reasonable expectations that she helps to clean up afterwards.

Do not be over-protective, wrapping your child in cotton wool to save him from the cruel world (see Parenting Myth No.5). Within commonsense limits, let him learn from the natural consequences of his own behaviour, rather than from an artificial punishment introduced by you after you have cleaned up his mess for him. If his behaviour is seriously threatening life or property, you will naturally intervene and prevent the unacceptable behaviour. But otherwise let your child learn that when he does silly or wrong things, there is probably a price he will have to pay.

Do not worry about when your child can count or say the alphabet (or read the encyclopaedia or compose her first symphony). As long as she seems to be understanding more language as time goes by, just accept that children develop at different rates. If she does not seem to be increasing her understanding, take her for a check-out.

Do not try to rush toilet training. The nerves necessary to have voluntary control don't mature until about two so real toilet training can't occur before that. You can sometimes get a primitive form of conditioning at a younger age, but often at great emotional expense. I have suggested an approach to toilet-training below.

Helping children to improve their behaviour

Children are mostly fun and mostly rewarding, most of the time. But sometimes they are a pain in the neck, unpleasant and unreasonable. Even if you are faithfully following all of my suggestions above, you will still probably strike the normal problems of normal childhood, such as the occasional tantrum, teasing or non-compliance with a reasonable request from you. If you think your child, now meaning from about one to twelve years of age, is consistently behaving in some unacceptable ways, there are some basic steps you can take to help him improve his behaviour. If the problem seems beyond a self-help approach, or it doesn't improve, do get some help from a qualified clinical psychologist.

Step 1   Define the problem

Pinpoint exactly what your child does or doesn't do that is a problem. Make sure you are describing his behaviour not your interpretation of it. For example, 'The problem is he teases his younger sister' or 'The problem is she won't accept reasonable requests from her mother' *not* 'The problem is he is aggressive' or 'The problem is she is trying to make me look foolish'. Discuss the problem with your spouse to see whether you agree there is a real problem. You will both need to be involved in any behaviour-improvement programme, so you both need to agree on its need.

If you agree this is a problem that should be tackled, explain to your child calmly and quietly exactly what she is doing wrong and why it is unacceptable, indicating clearly how you want her to behave instead. Even young children can understand such an explanation, although you may need to repeat it a few times. Levelling and requesting is the appropriate formula. For example, 'When you tease your sister, she gets upset and that's unpleasant for all of us, so I don't like it. If she annoys you, I want you to come and tell me, okay?' Or, 'When you won't pick up your toys like I ask, it makes more work for me and I feel very angry about that. I would like you to pick up your toys when I ask, please.'

Step 2   Count the behaviour

You will remember that goals are measurable so that you can tell how far you have progressed towards them and exactly when they have been achieved. Now your goal is to help your child improve his behaviour, and the same need exists, which is why you needed a precise definition of the problem. Keeping a careful record of how often the behaviour occurs will give you a benchmark to measure progress by. You can keep a tally, or even a graph, on his bedroom wall or in the kitchen. For example:

Day	Number of teasing bouts
Monday	4
Tuesday	3
Wednesday	5

Or:

Day	Number of requests refused
Saturday	6
Sunday	2

and so on.

Step 3   Identify possible rewards and penalties

First, are there apparent rewards for the unacceptable behaviour? For example, is he teasing his sister as a means of getting your attention? If there are rewards for the unacceptable behaviour, try to remove them. If your attention seems to have been a reward, in the future give only as much as is needed to implement this programme. But make sure you do pay attention when he behaves as you are requesting.

Second, what are possible rewards for improving his behaviour? A good rule of thumb is that anything your child does a lot is a possible reward. Try to match the 'size' of the reward to the difficulty of the improvement.

Third, what is a suitable penalty for not improving? Sometimes the natural consequences of the unacceptable behaviour will be sufficient punishment in themselves. Or you may use Time Out (explained below). Or you may use, or support Time Out with, the loss of some privilege, like an evening's television, or a reduction in pocket money.

Step 4   Contract for the desired improvement

I have already suggested you can use contracts as a motivational booster to help you achieve your goals; now you can share that technique with your child. In a family discussion involving your child and preferably both parents, explain what is unacceptable about his present behaviour and agree on the goals for improvement. Spell out the rewards he can earn and the penalties he will pay, depending on his behaviour. Write out the contract. For example: 'Each day that Charlie does not tease his sister, he earns one star on his tally chart. At the end of the week, if he has at least five stars, Dad will take him bike-riding in the park. If Charlie does tease his sister, he will immediately go to Time Out and he earns a cross for that day on his tally chart. At the end of the week, if he has more than three crosses, he is not allowed to watch television on Saturday afternoon.' Pin up the contract where it can be seen, as a reminder of the goal for improvement and so that there can be no argument about what was agreed.

Step 5   Try out the contract

The most common reason for contracting not working with children is that the parents are inconsistent. Once you break the contract or allow your child to, don't be surprised if it loses its effectiveness. It is not unusual to need to adjust a contract, to make or maintain its effectiveness. The improvement or rewards or penalties may be too big or too little. Or you may wish to set sub-goals along the way to a large improvement, and so need to keep raising the standard for a reward. Remember the contract is a motivational aid to help your child improve her behaviour in an agreed way, so involve her in discussing any adjustments to the contract so that it is as helpful to her as it can be.

Step 6   Fade out the contract

Your long-term goal is self-directed, successful behaviour in your child. Contracting is an interim measure to help your child develop that, and it should be gradually faded out. This involves handing over control of the contract to your child, the extent depending on his age and ability to administer it. Older children should be able to run the whole contract themselves eventually. When your child is running as much of the contract as she can, ask her to tell you when she thinks she no longer needs it, to support her improved behaviour. Remember, it was an aid to help her improve her behaviour, so she decides when she no longer needs that aid. However, you can help him to maintain his improved behaviour by attending to and praising it, long after the contract has been dropped.

This hand over of control is done in several stages. To begin, you administer the contract by counting the behaviours, keeping the records, and handing out the rewards or penalties. When that is all running smoothly, ask your child to count the behaviours, while you do the rest. When he is doing the counting well, ask him to keep the records, and finally he will administer his own rewards and penalties. In case you are worried that your child will cheat, bear in mind two things. First, you have to make yourself vulnerable in relationships in order to build trust: you have to give your kid the chance to cheat so she can show you that she doesn't. Second, the research on contracting shows that the children are usually much tougher on themselves than the adults would be.

If there are several problem behaviours you want to help your child improve, it's usually best to focus on only one or two at a time, so start with the most troublesome. Once that has improved, you may find other problems have disappeared, or you can tackle them next. Don't underestimate the practical value of contracting to help children improve their behaviour. By now, literally thousands of parents have used it successfully. If you are again falling victim to some of the old objections to contracting, like seeing it as 'bribery', you had better go back and review the discussion in Chapter 7.

Time out for humane punishment

I think there would be something essentially barbaric in someone of my size hitting someone of my son's size. I think justifying that assault by the fact that we are related and 'I'm only doing it for his good' would be a feeble excuse for my lack of self-control and effective parenting skills. In my earlier discussion of the Myths of Parenthood I pointed out that attempts to control your child with threats of physical or emotional violence are ineffective, obtaining at best an illusion of compliance while you're around and a return to unacceptable behaviour as soon as your back is turned. Often when I am discussing these issues with groups of parents, someone will say, 'I can see you are right, but surely there isn't any harm in giving him a smack when he's naughty.'

Well, there probably isn't any long-term harm in the *occasional* smack, but there isn't any good, either, for both of you. Psychologists at the University of Houston studied parents who either routinely used physical discipline (such as a smack on the hand), or occasionally used physical discipline (such as after talking had not worked), or never used physical discipline. In both the long and short term, physical discipline was unsuccessful. Toddlers who were smacked by their mothers were actually *more* likely again to grab breakable objects and *less* likely to obey restrictions. It was also noted by the psychologists that parents who relied on physical discipline were more likely to offer their children restricted environments with fewer safe or acceptable objects for play, with the resulting developmental drawbacks you would expect from our discussion above of the Missouri research.

So, if you shouldn't hit when your child plays up, what should you do? Send her to Time Out. In my advice in Chapter 4 for conflict resolution, I suggested you prevent a discussion from escalating into an argument by taking time out to cool down. When applied to your relationship with your child, Time Out again gives you both time to cool down. But it is also punishing your child for unacceptable behaviour by obliging him to take Time Out from pleasant and rewarding activity and do something boring instead. Time Out can take some time and persistence on your part to implement, more so if your child has become very practised at her unacceptable behaviour. Initially he may try to buck the system because he quite correctly recognizes he is losing some of his control over you. Stick to your guns and be consistent, and you will be surprised how well you can eliminate an unacceptable behaviour.

Step 1   Choose a location for time out

This should be somewhere bland and boring, away from other people. The problem with bedrooms is that they often contain toys and other interesting things. Many parents find the bathroom is the best location, putting bottles of shampoo and other potential toys in a plastic box that can be easily removed when your child goes into Time Out. The location should *not* be frightening; *never* lock your child in a room and do switch on the light if it's dark.

Step 2   Explain time out to your child

By now you should already have had a calm, family discussion explaining exactly what your child does that is unacceptable and why. You may well be introducing a contract to help her to improve her behaviour. You now explain that you are also going to use Time Out to help her. This means that in the future if she does the unacceptable behaviour, she must take herself to the Time Out location for the amount of time you specify. This will usually be two minutes. If she does not go immediately to Time Out when asked, the time becomes three minutes. If she still does not go, it becomes four minutes. If she still does not go, she then incurs a significant loss of privileges, such as no television or no pocket money for a week (use the penalties you have already worked out for ideas).

Time Out does not have to be long to be effective; research has found that four minutes works as well as forty, and it's a lot easier to administer. You can use a kitchen timer, setting it for the appropriate duration and telling your child he can come out of Time Out when the timer rings. The exception to this procedure is when the unacceptable behaviour is a temper tantrum or prolonged whingeing. Then the exit rule is that he can come out when he stops the unacceptable behaviour. Yes, he may carry on in there for some little time. That's still more pleasant than having him learn he can behave like that right next to your ear and that it is an effective way of making you do what he wants.

Step 3   Use time out

The next time the unacceptable behaviour occurs, calmly but firmly send your child to Time Out, adding one minute penalties if she

MANAGING THE NORMAL PROBLEMS OF NORMAL CHILDHOOD

Non-compliance
Contract for compliance; Time Out for non-compliance.

Teasing
Contract for not teasing; Time Out for teasing.

Toilet training in 3-year-olds
Contract for bathroom use; make your child responsible for rinsing training pants (with your help); do *not* scold or punish.

Bed wetting
Contract for dry bed; make your child responsible for changing wet bedding (with your help); do *not* scold or punish.

Temper tantrums
Time Out for tantrums (until the tantrum is over); model levelling for expressing bad feelings and contract for it instead of tantrums.

Child intruding into parents' bed
Contract for staying in her own bed (except when allowed into yours, and make that clear and consistent).

Whingeing and whining
Time Out for whingeing or whining; model levelling and making requests and contract for those behaviours instead of whingeing or whining.

Going to bed
Contract for going to bed at the agreed time; Time Out for not going; it helps to give a half-hour signal of approaching bedtime, to help your child wind down and wrap up any activity.

---

does not comply, backing that up with a loss of privileges if necessary. *Never* take your child to Time Out by force; that's just slipping back into physical punishment and starting a battle of strength that eventually you must lose. Just stick to your guns and calmly keep reflecting to your child that his non-compliance is just costing him more.

When your child does something else unacceptable, you should level then about why it is unacceptable and make a clear request for what you want her to do instead. At that point you can announce that Time Out will apply to any further occurrences of the behaviour, but it's unfair and unrealistic to use it the first time. Time Out is to help your child improve his behaviour, not for you to vent your anger or get revenge.

Like contracting, Time Out has now been used successfully by thousands of parents. Dr Gerry Patterson, from Oregon University, has suggested combinations of these two techniques for managing the 'normal problems of normal childhood', which I have summarized in the table on page 165. I repeat, the main requirement for success with these techniques is consistency, and they will not compensate for serious problems in the parents, their relationship or the child. If you think you have tried them consistently and they are not working, it's time to see a qualified clinical psychologist.

Successfully surviving adolescence

It is an obvious fact, easily overlooked by the parents of teenagers, that adolescence is eminently survivable, for both kids and parents. In the middle of it, you can lose sight of that fact, usually because of growing conflict around the issue of independence. Teenagers' parents are very prone to fall into the parental myths about controlling their children's behaviour 'for their good', while the adolescents quite correctly realise they are involved in the important task of developing their independence. Result: World War III, or so it can seem.

The typical points of conflict between parents and adolescents are:

curfew (what time to be home);
personal hygiene and dress;
choice of friends;
chores;
homework;
room tidiness;
parental authority.

If you read this list thoughtfully, bearing the Parenting Myths in mind, you will have to agree that many of these issues are not worth much conflict. It may be embarrassing or distasteful to you if your teenager wants to dress like a shop dummy or to have a hair style that looks as if he has used his head for cleaning paint brushes, but since you don't control his behaviour you are not responsible for it. Being over-worried about being judged on your children's appearance or behaviour says something about *your* self-esteem.

Naturally not all of the above issues can be dismissed with resigned tolerance. I have already suggested how you can most effectively encourage your child to do well at study. If you want her to learn how to live successfully in a drug-using society (like ours), recognize the overriding importance of your modelling, and set an example of sensible drug use. Back this up by levelling on how you feel about drugs and being willing to listen to his viewpoint, and you will be as influential as possible. If you want her to learn how to express her sexuality successfully and responsibly, bear in mind the consistent research finding that that is the usual outcome of honest sex education, and make sure some of that occurs at home. If you have postponed your attempts at sex education with your children until they are teenagers, then you have effectively spent some years teaching them this is a topic you don't discuss. Don't be surprised if they have learned that lesson and reject your initiative now. You can still make sure they have access to appropriate reading and emphasise your availability to talk, when they want to. Parents are the prime sex educators of their children whether they recognize that or not, as I pointed out in a previous chapter. I encourage you to recognize that and have a good try at doing it successfully.

If you can accept that you never really had control over your children's behaviour, least of all now that they are teenagers, and that what you do have is influence, then the name of the game is how do you exert maximum influence in what you see as desirable directions. And the answers you have already read: clear, prompt, non-defensive and non-aggressive communication and conflict-resolution (Chapter 4); a mutually respectful, assertive approach, based on making requests, negotiating around them, and constructively solving problems together (Chapter 5); and throughout, realistic expectations of yourself and your children (this chapter). My discussion of successful parenting with adolescents is shorter than those with toddlers and children, not because it is any less important, but because we have already largely covered the topic.

If your children are young or non-existent yet, you have the advantage of a head start. You can begin implementing all of the above suggestions and you will find my recipe for successfully surviving adolescence comes reasonably easily. If your children are already teenagers, and you have followed few of my suggestions in this chapter so far, then you are probably sitting there thinking it's a pie-in-the-sky notion that only a psychologist could dream up. Well, it's never too late to try. You have a far better chance of obtaining improvement in a relationship if both (or all) of the people involved are working together in the same direction.

So share this book. 'I'm very unhappy about the way we have been arguing a lot lately and I would like things to improve. I have been reading this book with some ideas about how parents and teenagers can communicate and get on better, and it makes sense to me. I would appreciate it if you would read the chapters I have marked. Then let's talk it over and give it a try.' Sure, you will probably feel embarrassed making such an approach, and you would all feel awkward trying out the new interpersonal skills. No one ever died of embarrassment or awkwardness and that's a small price to pay for better family relationships, more real influence with your kids, and successful adolescents.

However, if the conflict has reached the point where you cannot co-operate on a self-help project like that, then again it's time to see a qualified clinical psychologist. Some of the families I see are able to retrieve the situation; some are not. Do your personal, realistic best to make a success of this important part of your life, but accept the realistic limitations on you.